THE VIKING RUNES *Traditional Meanings*

ᛗ	the Self	Man, the Human Race
ᚷ	Partnership	A gift, Offerings from the gods or from Chiefs to Loyal Followers
ᚠ	Signals	God, the god Loki, Mouth (source of Divine Utterances), Rivermouth
ᛜ	Retreat	Property or Inherited Possessions, also Native Land, Home
ᚢ	Strength	Strength, Sacrificial Animal, the Aurochs (*bos primigenius*), species of wild ox
ᚲ	Initiation	Uncertain Meaning, a Secret Matter (Rune of Mystery)
ᚾ	Constraint	Need, Necessity, Constraint, Cause of Human Sorrow, Lessons, Hardship
ᛝ	Fertility	Ing, the Legendary Hero, later a god
ᛇ	Defense	Yew-tree, a Bow Made of Yew, Rune Magic, Avertive Powers: Runic Calendars or "Primstaves"
ᛉ	Protection	Protection, Defense, the Elk, Sedge or Eelgrass
ᚨ	Possessions	Cattle, Goods, the Vital Community Wealth
ᚹ	Joy	Joy, also in *Cynewulf's* Runic Passages, Absence of Suffering & Sorrow
ᛜ	Harvest	Year, Harvest, A Fruitful Year
ᚲ	Opening	Torch, Skiff, Ulcer, Associated with Cult of the Goddess Nerthus
ᛏ	Warrior	Victory in Battle, a Guiding Planet or Star, the god Tiw
ᛒ	Growth	Birch Tree, Associated with Fertility Cults, Rebirth, New Life
ᛗ	Movement	Horse, Associated with the Course of the Sun
ᚱ	Flow	Water, Sea, a Fertility Source (See Grendel's Mere in *Beowulf*)
ᚻ	Disruption	Hail, Sleet, Natural Forces that Damage
ᚱ	Journey	A Riding, a Journey: Refers to the Soul After Death, Journey Charm
ᚦ	Gateway	Giant, Demon, Thorn, the god Thor
ᛞ	Breakthrough	Day, God's Light, Prosperity and Fruitfulness
ᛁ	Standstill	Ice, Freezing, in the *Prose Edda* the Frost-giant Ymir is Born of Ice
ᛋ	Wholeness	The Sun
ᚺ	the unknowable	The Rune of Destiny

The Book
of
RuneCards

Also by the author:

The Book of Runes
Rune Play

The Book of RuneCards

Sacred Play for Self-Discovery

Commentary by
Ralph Blum

ORACLE BOOKS
ST. MARTIN'S PRESS
NEW YORK

Grateful acknowledgment is made for permission to reprint from "The RuneCard Meditations," © 1988 by Ralph Blum.

Library of Congress Cataloging-in-Publication Data
Blum, Ralph.
     The book of runecards : sacred play for self-discovery / Ralph Blum.
        p. cm.
     Companion vol. to: The book of runes.
     "Oracle Books"
     ISBN 0-312-03423-7
     1. Runes—Miscellanea. 2. Oracles I. Title.
BF1779.R86B57 1989
133.3'3—dc20   89-30428
                                           CIP

First Edition
10 9 8 7 6 5 4 3 2 1

Edited by Bronwyn Jones
Illustrations by Jancis Salerno
Design by Susan Hood

To all who serve the Divine,
in themselves and in others,
this work is dedicated.

The Three Norns, or goddesses of Fate, live under the *Yggdrasil,* the Tree of Life, where they weave the web of fate and guard the golden apples from which the gods receive experience, knowledge and eternal youth. *Urd,* the wise and ancient Norn, teaches

lessons of the past, while *Verdandi,* who is young, fearless and straightforward, bids good use of the present, and *Skuld,* who is closely veiled, warns the gods of future evil.

CONTENTS

ACKNOWLEDGMENTS

To Bronwyn Jones, friend and editor, who for eleven years has shared her wisdom with me. There are many styles in creative partnerships. Ours is one of the highest.

To Jane Walmsley for her patience and skill in creating the images for the RuneCards.

To Jancis Salerno, whose graceful illustrations for this present work, like those provided for *The Book of Runes,* leave nothing to be desired.

To Joan Halifax for her friendship and her insight in linking the Native American Indian Medicine Wheel and the Viking Runes.

To Alfred Paxton Lowman, the kind of Spiritual Warrior to have for a friend at any time, and particularly at negotiation time.

To Nancy Shaw, Robert Lee O'Hare, Dean Loomos and all the staff at the RuneWorks for keeping the ship afloat while I was in my cave.

To everyone at St. Martin's Press—from the second floor to the eighteenth—for making this project possible. In particular, to Barbara Andrews, Holly Bash, David Stanford

Burr, Andy Carpenter, Maureen Delaney, Chona Denusta, Tom Dunne, Stephanie Dyson, Joe Fergis, Roy Gainsburg, Robert Gong, David Kaye, Patti Hughes, Hank Jones, Amelie Littell, Josh Marwell, Tom McCormack, Tim McGuire, Helen Plog, Frank Rolfe, Phil Schwartz, Robert Weil, and to my many friends and allies among the St. Martin's sales force.

I owe a special debt of gratitude to my friend David Hirshfeld, St. Martin's Assistant Editor and band nurse for *The RuneCards.*

And finally, to all the people who use the Viking Runes, and who have shared with us their experiences and insights.

Guð blessi ykkur!

PREFACE

Deep in the collective unconscious of humanity—and perhaps in its very heart—lies the desire to worship a revealing God who will disclose to believers everything they need to know for living a full and productive life.

And to that end, each religion has a place for the oracular. An Oracle can be a Divine saying and/or a vehicle for discerning Divine Wisdom. The *Urim* and *Thummin* of the Old Testament are translated as "Lights and Perfections." They have been described as two gemstones placed on the breastplate of the high priest and used in an oracular manner to discern Jehovah's will in difficult decisions. The Oracle was employed by the priest to discover Jehovah's wishes for the people in their going out and their coming in, to discover whether to begin or end an activity. In other words, *Urim* and *Thummin* were used to bring revelation to life from start to finish.

In the New Testament, the Greek word for the oracular is *logia,* meaning short sayings or communications from God, as well as the process or channels through which God reveals Himself. The choosing of a disciple to replace Judas Iscariot was accomplished by oracular means—the drawing of lots.

Considering all the above, I now come to Ralph Blum and the Runes. Are they, the Runes, Lights and Perfections of the Divine? Or are they of divination? Divination is explained in Deuteronomy 18:10–12 as: observers of times, enchanters, witches, charmers, consultants of familiar spirits, wizards, all of which are an abomination of the Lord.

I take Scripture seriously and eschew horoscopes, channeling, palm reading and the like. Any knowledge that is secret and privy to a select few concerning things of the future, I reject. Moreover, I have been very suspicious, as an Evangelical Christian, of any vehicle which claims to have special wisdom from the Divine, wisdom which I cannot ascertain from my prayer life with the Holy Spirit. My first and second impression of the Runes was one of dismissal. I saw them as a pagan, ancient tool of superstition for insecure people.

And yet, over the twenty-five years that Ralph Blum and I have loved each other as brothers, I have watched his quest and pilgrimage to discern the *Urim, Logia,* and Wisdom of the Divine. That odyssey has taken him to strange places and ancient practices of the oracular. I have watched him order all these experiences in light of the Scriptures. His journey toward the oracular has been a genuine quest, full of humility and spiritual hunger. And I watched that journey bring him to the Runes.

So how can I resolve my deep distrust of divination with my deep love for Ralph Blum? This was my particular dilemma when I visited him in January, 1989. I was acutely aware of my discomfort as I walked the beach in Malibu that first evening. Later I studied the Scriptures, then slept restlessly all night at his home over the water and sand. The next morning I arose with confidence, at peace with my answer.

The word came from I Peter 4:11. The text became for me a litmus test for the legitimacy of the Runes. To paraphrase I Peter: *All things oracular must be used to the end that God may be glorified in all things.* Peter counseled Christians to use the oracular with gravity and authority, as a transmission of divine truth rather than for the gratification of personal desires.

What words of wisdom! Good counsel for any reader, especially for this suspicious yet loving friend of Ralph Blum. Listen: I am persuaded that God desires His Will to be made known to creation. To do less is to honor darkness rather than light. I am convinced that Divine Will *is* discernable, and that the map God reveals to us supports our *stand in the present* and our *walk in the future.* Divination and magic and secret knowledge be gone! I intend to attend to the Divine. My prayer for you who are practitioners of the Runes is that you will use this oracular device with gravity and authority.

I have shared with you my own personal wrestling match in hopes that you might journey with me to a deeper appreciation of the oracular, and perhaps, the Runes. My journey, Ralph knows, has often been painful as I seek to grow from knowing self to knowing God.

I am not yet a disciple of the Runes. I am, however, a

loving disciple of God, His *Urim, Logia,* and Wisdom. For me, then, the oracular *is* scriptural. As such, it need not be limited and sealed within the sacred texts of the first century, let alone buried with the Germanic and Viking traditions. The Divine lives and so does The Word.

Dr. Wallace K. Reid
Pastor Emeritus,
Chester Congregational Church
Chester, Vermont

The Sandnes Christ, Iceland ca. 1300 A.D.

INVOCATION

I honor your gods.
I drink at your well.
I bring an undefended heart
    to our meeting place.
I have no cherished outcomes.
I will not negotiate by withholding.
I am not subject to disappointment.

INTRODUCTION

ORACLE, *from the Latin* oraculum, *divine announcement . . . 1. among the ancient Greeks and Romans, a) the place where or medium by which deities were consulted; b) the revelation or response of a medium or priest; 2. a) any person or agency believed to be in communication with a deity; b) any person of great knowledge or wisdom; c) opinions or statements of any such oracle; 3. the holy of holies of the ancient Jewish Temple.*

—Webster's New World Dictionary

And the oracle he prepared in the house within, to set there the ark of the covenant of the Lord.

—I Kings 6:19

People all over this country, from all walks of life, are experiencing the intense desire to be filled by Spirit. We are being moved to become, in our own right, oracular voices for a power greater than ourselves. What we are seeing, in all its various manifestations in contemporary American society, is what British scholar John Michell calls "the reenchantment of our nature."

Moreover, we are living in a time when secret teachings are at last being made available to the general public. Perhaps today's thoughtful shamans and wisdom bearers feel that if they *don't* do something, we may not long endure. Or perhaps the elders have decided that, with advances in media and communication, the means are now available to get the message out, so why not? At any rate, there has been a shift. Shamans are talking, selectively opening the vaults and archives of sacred wisdom to those outside tribal circles. We and our children are the beneficiaries of this new openness.

Simultaneously, there is a growing interest in traditional folkways and ancient traditions like the oracular. With each passing year, the Viking Runes are gaining wider acceptance. Available to a growing audience since 1982, the Runes are proving helpful to therapists and members of various Twelve-Step Programs, as well as to religious leaders of different persuasions and measures of tolerance. People from all walks of life, living on three continents, and coming from a broad spectrum of ethnic backgrounds, have found the Runes to be user-friendly and spiritually sound.

The purpose of this book is akin to that of *The Book of Runes*—to reintroduce an ancient Oracle, the Runes. Both works are intended as handbooks for the Spiritual Warrior:

> Free of anxiety, radically alone and unattached to outcomes, the Spiritual Warrior practices absolute trust in the struggle for awareness, and is constantly mindful that what matters is to have a *true present*. It takes a long time to grow in wisdom, to say nothing of the time it takes to learn to think well. Following the Warrior Way is not for everyone, although it is available to all who are willing to undergo its challenges. To embark on this path is to cultivate the Witness Self, the Watcher

Within, the one who can profitably converse with the Runes.*

Perhaps the most powerful feature of the Runes as an Oracle is their potential use as an *intuitive trainer.* Western cultures are largely deficient in skills for training the right hemisphere, the part of the brain responsible for nonlinear imaginative thinking, the part that Benedictine theologian Father Bede Griffiths describes as housing "the other half of the soul." I suggest that it is our capacity for Intuitive Knowing which is addressed in Scripture with the commanding words *Be still and know that I am God.* It may be that the training of Sacred Intuition—a new way of listening for that Inner Voice—is the primary function of the Runes.

When I initially encountered the Runes, I did not realize that there was a traditional alphabetic sequence that had not been modified in nearly two thousand years. A trip to the local library could have set me straight. But it was the middle of the night when I first began to play with the Runes, and the Xeroxed pages on which their symbols had come to me were unnumbered. Not knowing which page came first, or even if it mattered, I left it to the Runes to put themselves into a sequence that suited *them.*

Needless to say, my reordering of the traditional runic alphabet has not amused the scholarly community. In 1984, however, I visited Professor Sven Janssen, Sweden's leading runologist, at his summer home. I showed him *The Book of Runes* and explained that I had let the runic alphabet reorder itself. After watching me demonstrate how I use the

*Ralph Blum, *The Book of Runes* (New York: St. Martin's Press, 1983), p. 13.

Oracle, he patted me on the shoulder and said in a consoling voice, "Never mind what the academicians say. Your version of the alphabet may prove useful to people in their lives."

The Runes as Visual Metaphors

Now, the time has come to take the work of contemporary runecraft a step further, to translate the glyphs or symbols, with their tapestry of ancient meanings, into visual metaphors. And so, calling upon the remarkable skill of English artist and illustrator Jane Walmsley, a first attempt has been made to clothe the stark runic symbols in evocative images—the RuneCards.

Almost five years have gone into designing, modifying and testing the RuneCards. From the beginning, Jane and I worked together. We spent many hours talking over each of the runic glyphs with its primary and extended meanings. Then Jane set about bringing the images into focus. Once the design had come to suit her, she would send the card-in-progress to me in the United States for my response. A number of the images appear on the cards exactly as she first conceived them. Certain of the images have been revised more times than either of us cares to remember. But for now, at least, we have made peace with our hesitations. The deck is complete.

It was my intention, when I first discussed the art for the RuneCards with Jane, not to have the glyphs stand out too boldly. Rather, I hoped that, wherever possible, the runic symbols might be embedded in the designs and disguised in a subtle fashion. Thanks to Jane's imaginative efforts, six of the cards achieve this effect. In one of the RuneCards the glyph actually appears twice.

The two Runes that gave us the greatest difficulty were *Laguz,* the Rune of Flow, and *Dagaz,* the Rune of Breakthrough and Transformation:

18. *Flow*   22. *Breakthrough*

The art for both cards went through many permutations. *Flow* wouldn't flow, and *Transformation* was a long time in coming.

On the one hand, *Flow* carries the most feminine feeling of all the Runes. In it the "creative and fertile powers of Nature" are at work; powers whose attributes are "water, fluidity, the ebb and flow of tides and emotions." The possible images for *Flow* moved across the landscape, under the sea, even into space before finally settling where land and sea meet, in the sand of the shoreline.

The language of *Breakthrough,* on the other hand, is marked by more active, masculine phrases: "major shift . . . complete transformation . . . 180-degree turn . . . radical trust." The rejected art for *Dagaz* included stone monuments, ancient artifacts, austere landscapes. The last drawing to be discarded, a leafless forest at dawn, led to the final vision of *Breakthrough.*

In the texts that accompany the many available tarot decks, you will often find exhaustive interpretations of the cards' symbolism. With the RuneCards, however, it was my decision not to lock the reader into any one set of meanings. Instead, you are asked to meditate on the images and allow the interpretations to arise directly from your Intuitive Knowing. Each time you turn to the RuneCards, approach them with open mind and heart, and allow the images to speak to you.

Innovations and Resources

Before preparing this edition of *The Book of RuneCards,* I decided to test the waters. A limited edition of one thousand decks was offered to those on The RuneWorks' mailing list. With that edition was included a small booklet containing twenty-five brief meditations upon the images, intended as a contemporary echo of the ancient Rune poems. These poems are included with the Rune Interpretations in this volume.

The Interpretations for the twenty-five cards are essentially the same as they were in *The Book of Runes.* The remainder of the text, however, is new. Four chapters—Runes and Healing; Runes and Dreaming; The Cycle of Initiation; and Runes, Faith and Prediction—provide rich new areas for experimentation. In addition to these chapters, there are a number of exercises and ceremonies designed especially for the RuneCards, all of which may be usefully undertaken with the Rune stones as well.

The ceremony called *The Wheel of Initiation* draws on the thirteen cards of the *Cycle of Initiation* first introduced in *The Book of Runes.* Anthropologist Joan Halifax and I created this ceremony in the spring of 1987 as we sat together in a sunny courtyard in San Cristobal de las Casas in Chiapas,

Mexico. The Wheel of Initiation lends itself particularly well to the laying out of cards and is constructed on a Native American Indian mandala, the Medicine Wheel.

Since *The Book of RuneCards* will serve many of you as a first introduction to the Viking Runes, I have included a historical chapter to provide a perspective on the rise, fall and return of the Oracle. For readers who wish to gain a broader knowledge of classical runology, the works of R. W. V. Elliott, R. I. Page, Sir David Wilson and Magnus Magnusson are recommended. One of the most creative contemporary books on runecraft is *Rune Games* by Marijane Osborn and Stella Longland. This and other useful books are listed in the Bibliography.

For those of you interested in the ongoing tradition of Odinism and other formalist practices, I can highly recommend the scholarly works by my friend Edred Thorsson. As for myself, I am not an admirer of the magical or the occult. My concern is with the oracular tradition and with providing tools and techniques to tap into the ever-present wisdom of the Divine Within.

Many aspects of ancient runecraft will never be known with any kind of certainty. My study of the Runes has convinced me that their roots go far deeper than scholars have allowed. And yet, independent of its history, there is always an appropriateness that connects a true Oracle to any age that finds reason to honor it. As suggested in *The Book of Runes,* "function determines form, use confers meaning, and an Oracle always resonates to the requirements of the time in which it is consulted." And, let me add, to the requirements of the person consulting it. The renewed interest in the Runes is creating its own history and tradition in this our time.

Omens, Portents and Paradoxes

As is my custom, before beginning to write, I consulted the Runes concerning the timeliness of this new work. I shuffled the deck and drew one card. To my surprise, it was ⋈, *Hagalaz,* the Rune of Disruption and Elemental Power—what I think of as the Rune of "radical discontinuity."

I didn't turn at once to the interpretation for the nineteenth Rune. Instead, in my mind, I returned to the farmhouse in New Milford, Connecticut, where I first began working with the Runes. I was alone again in my study, listening to the sound of peepers in the hot darkness. One by one, I held the Rune stones in my hand, meditating on their meanings, writing down the thoughts that came to me. . . .

Certainly what happened on that far-off summer's night epitomized the action of *Hagalaz.* My life was changed forever. What I once regarded as disruption, I now see as a necessary and positive part of our existence. Disruption serves those who, in their love of the Divine, welcome the tests and challenges that are sent to them. Invention, freedom and change are among the hallmarks of this Rune. Liberation from our cherished material reality, release into the rhythms of Divine Mind—these are signals of *Hagalaz* in action. *Everything changes* is the sweet refrain that sings beneath the dissonant chords of Disruption.

I am a great fan of omens, portents and paradoxes. It pleases me to look back over the weave and discover, in the earlier lay of threads and colors, the hint of themes yet to be developed.

In 1986, I was in Australia visiting reef biologist Walter Starck on his research vessel, the *El Torrito.* One night, anchored out on the Great Barrier Reef, Walt pointed out a constellation called "The Phoenix," which is visible only in the Southern Hemisphere.

I forgot about that conversation until two years later when artist Jane Walmsley finally came up with the image for the twenty-fifth Rune Card. We had talked a lot about how to envision that which, by its intrinsic nature, is unknowable. She handed me her picture of a night sky with stars and asked me if I recognized the star group. I said I didn't. "You can't see it from the Northern Hemisphere," Jane said. "It's called the Phoenix."

The memory of those long-ago nights fades. For the first time in perhaps an hour, I was conscious of the sound of the surf. The tide had turned and was coming in. I was seated at my desk in Malibu on a sunny January afternoon. The RuneCards lay beside the computer, *Disruption* on top. As I carry forward my work the RuneCards, I am once again prepared to welcome *Hagalaz* into my life.

I got up and walked out onto the deck just in time to see a solitary dolphin break the surface thirty yards offshore. How comforting it is to receive a favorable sign at the beginning of a long voyage.

Learning new ways to use the Runes is akin to being parachuted into a strange land. The climate is inviting, the terrain often breathtaking, there is plenty of time to explore. After all, when an Oracle has been around for more than two millennia, why hurry? Over the years, we at the RuneWorks have learned much from your letters. We appreciate the interchange and hope to hear of your experiences with the RuneCards. As time passes, working with the Runes becomes more and more a collaborative venture.

This new volume is an invitation to you to try novel ways of consulting the Runes. Whether cut into stone or engraved on paper, the function of the Runes is limited only by your imagination. And so I offer *The Book of Rune-Cards* to novices and veteran users alike in the earnest hope that they may serve you and, in so doing, enable you to serve the highest good, the Will of the Divine.

A GAELIC BLESSING

Deep peace of the running wave to you.
Deep peace of the flowing air to you.
Deep peace of the quiet earth to you.
Deep peace of the shining stars to you.
Deep peace of the gentle night to you.
Moon and stars pour their healing light on you.
Deep peace of the Light of the World to you.

Burial Stone, North Jutland,
Denmark, circa 1150 A.D.

I

THE RETURN OF A WESTERN ORACLE

I beseech the immaculate Master of Monks
To steer my journeys;
May the Lord of the lofty heavens
Hold His strong arm over me. . . .

> —Oldest surviving Christian verse-prayer in Icelandic;
> composed by a Hebridean poet during the colonizing
> voyage of Eirik the Red from Iceland to Greenland.

I see a black sail on the horizon
   set under a dark cloud that hides the sun. . . .
Bring me my Broadsword and clear understanding
Bring me my cross of gold as a talisman
Bless with a hard heart those who surround me
Bless the women and children who firm our hands
Put our backs to the North wind. Hold fast by the river
Sweet memories to drive us on for the Motherland.

> —Jethro Tull, "Broadsword"

An air of mystery will always surround the origins and sacred use of the Runes. The word itself means a "secret" or "mystery" and is associated with things whispered. Out of their Latin and Etruscan

3

origins, and influenced by the dialects of the north Italian hill peoples, came the Runes, a twenty-four-letter alphabetic script created among the Germanic tribes at least two thousand years ago.

The resulting alphabet, which incorporated fertility symbols from prehistoric rock carvings, was linked from the outset to religious beliefs and ritual practices. Although never a spoken language, the Runes do comprise a symbolic system whose sacred function was to permit communication between humankind and the gods. The traditions of *runemal,* the art of Rune casting, were transmitted orally by *legomonism,* the passing on of sacred knowledge from master to apprentice through initiation. However, as the knowledge of the Runes spread, so did their use in poetry, for memorials to the dead, and for commerce and trade.

By the fourth century A.D., the Runes were becoming widely known in northern Europe, carried from place to place by traders and adventurers, warriors and even, in time, by Anglo-Saxon missionaries. For this to happen, a common alphabet was required—the alphabet that became known as *futhark* after its first six letters:

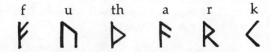

f   u   th   a   r   k

The original Germanic or Elder Futhark is comprised of twenty-four letters and was probably in existence as early as the second century B.C. The later or Younger Futhark was reduced to sixteen letters by the ninth century A.D., while later Anglo-Saxon futhark alphabets expanded to include as many as thirty-three letters.

The Elder Futhark was divided into three "families" of eight Runes each, which were named for the Norse gods *Freyr, Hagal* and *Tyr.*

Freyr's Eight:

Hagal's Eight:

Tyr's Eight:

In the ancient runic alphabet each symbol or glyph possessed a signifying sound and a meaningful name. The "R" *(Raido)* meant a journey and also referred to the voyage of the soul after death. The "A" *(Ansuz)* was connected with signals and messages, and was associated with the mouth as a source of divine utterance, with the mouths of rivers, and with the Norse god Loki.

Certain of the Runes still bear traces of their ancient pictographic or ideographic origins, suggesting parallels with classical Chinese. The pictograph for "man" in Chinese, for instance, still resembles the human figure, standing upright, legs spread: 人 . Add one more brush stroke 大 and you have the ideograph for greatness, suggesting man and his greatness.

In the runic alphabet, the letter "Z" *(Algiz),* the Rune of Protection, looks like this: Y . Originally, one of the associations for *Algiz* was the horns of an elk, suggesting the proper boundaries between people, the appropriate distance, so to speak, between your horns and mine.

As you can see, the wealth of connotations connected to each letter places the runic alphabet in quite a different light from the stark templates of our twenty-six-letter English alphabet.

From the ninth through the twelfth centuries, the Runes were carried by the Norsemen to Anglo-Saxon England, to Iceland and wherever their long voyages took them. Rune carvings, testifying to the extent of the Norse expeditions, have been found as far afield as Russia, Constantinople, the Orkney Islands, Greenland and—there is mounting evidence—on the North American continent. Shaped by the tribal wisdom of the northern fertile crescent from which many of our ancestors came to the New World, the Viking Runes emerged.

The craft of runemal touched every aspect of life from the most sacred to the most practical. There were Runes to influence the weather, the tides, crops, matters of love and healing; there were Runes of fertility, cursing and removing curses, birth and death. Runic glyphs were carved onto bone, into pieces of hardwood or cut into leather. Examples of the Rune carvers' art on swords, amulets, rings, bracelets and drinking cups are to be found in many of the world's museums. The most enduring evidence of the Rune carvers' skill—memorials to Viking warriors—can still be seen on huge standing stones along the roads and in fields throughout Scandinavia.

Who cut Runes? At what point did the carving qualify as religious or magical? And who qualified for the title "Rune-master"? A passage from R. I. Page's *Introduction to English Runes* provides a helpful overview of the subject:

> In some cases the rune-master would be simply a monumental mason accustomed to cutting inscrip-

tions on stones and mastering runes as one of the scripts appropriate to his trade. In others he might be a literate Anglo-Saxon who found it convenient to express himself in runes. In others again a die-cutter who copied runes from an exemplar, a coin, another die, possibly a drawing presented to him by his employer. But if in early times runes were intimately connected with magic, a rune-master then would be an awesome figure. By his use of the symbols he would be in command of supernatural powers, enticing hidden forces into his service. It is this type of rune-master that has attracted and mis-led many scholars, and perhaps only this type truly deserves the title "rune-master."*

In the eighth-century Anglo-Saxon poem *Beowulf,* the Dan-ish nobleman Æschere is spoken of as the king's *runwita,* a title which qualified him as the king's confidant.

The richest find of Rune sticks, or *runakefli,* and other Rune carvings was made after a fire in 1955 that destroyed a large part of the Bryggen waterfront district in Bergen, Norway. The runakefli, their lettering usually cut with a knife, served as talismans, markers of possession, and often carried love letters. The Bryggen discovery contains a wealth of messages from business partners, drinking com-panions, sailors and lovers. One of the Rune sticks carries the plaintive "Ingebjorg loved me when I was in Sta-vanger." Concerning the diversity of inscriptions on Rune sticks found after the Bryggen fire, Elliott writes:

*R. I. Page, *An Introduction to English Runes* (London: Metheun, 1973), p. 117.

There are many instances among the Bergen runes of invocatory and talismanic import, including Christian prayers, Ave Marias, names of archangels, prayers for childbirth, some fifty futharks, a charm against hostile creatures which reads, "I cut runes of help, I cut runes of protection, once against the elves, twice against the trolls, thrice against the ogres." . . . The impression gained from a study of the Bergen runes is above all one of the diversity of uses to which runes were put during the later Viking centuries, mundane, magical, and Christian.[*]

Most of the runic artifacts that we now possess date from no later than the twelfth century. And yet, in Iceland, as late as the seventeenth century, people caught with Runes in their possession were still being burnt. The use of Runes in Iceland was officially forbidden in 1639.

The Period of the Dual Faith

Christianity was slow to take hold in the Norse countries. It was almost ten centuries after the birth of Christ before Denmark could be properly called a Christian country. Nor were the Norwegians in a rush to abandon their pagan beliefs. The conversion of Norway, credited to the "royal evangelist" King Olaf Haraldsson—St. Olaf, Norway's first saint and martyr—did not occur until the eleventh century. And it was not until the great pagan center

[*]Ralph W. V. Elliott, *Runes: An Introduction* (Manchester, England: Manchester University Press, 1989), pp. 93–4.

of worship at Uppsala was destroyed in the twelfth century that the Swedes finally embraced Christianity.

For some centuries, there existed a period known as the *dual faith,* a time when both paganism and Christianity continued to coexist harmoniously. There is the story of Helgi the Lean, an early ninth-century settler of Iceland, who believed in Christ but invoked Thor on sea-journeys and in moments of duress. It was Thor who guided Helgi to his new home in the north of Iceland, but Helgi named the place *Kristness* (Christ-ness).

Evidence of the dual faith is to be found in early Viking and Anglo-Saxon art, poetry and inscriptions. One of the great works of art from the period is the eighth-century Franks casket, now in the British Museum. Quite small (9 inches long, 5⅛ high, 7½ wide), the elegant whalebone casket is covered with carvings depicting scenes from both the Bible and Norse mythology, with inscriptions in Runes and Roman letters.

Franks Casket, eighth century, whalebone

A remarkable example of early eighth-century North-umbrian art is an eighteen-foot-tall stone cross, known as the Ruthwell Cross for the church where it still stands in Dumfriesshire, England. The principal inscription, intended to enhance the biblical scenes depicted on the cross, is in Runes. The lines are from an Old English poem, "The Dream of the Rood":

> *krist wæs on rodi*
> *hwethræ ther fusæ fêarran kwomu*
> *aththilæ til anum ic thæt bih(êald)*

Christ was on the Cross
Still, many came swiftly, journeying from afar,
Hurrying to the Prince. I beheld it all.

The poem's author is unknown. The speaker in the poem is the wood of the Cross.

As worship of the pagan gods fell into disfavor and was displaced by Christianity, the runic alphabet was supplanted by the ubiquitous Latin script. However, the Runes continued to survive. Calendars known as primstave, or *runstaf,* usually carved or burned into wooden staves or plates, persisted beyond the medieval period in Scandinavia. These calendars were used to mark church holy days as well as times for planting and harvest, serving in effect as both calendar and farmer's almanac.

In 1543, Mogens Gyldenstjerne, a Dutch admiral, is said to have kept his private journal in Runes. During the Thirty Years War, the Runes were employed by the Swedish General Jacob de la Gardie for sending coded military messages, much as the United States used Native American Navajo speakers in the South Pacific during World War II.

Primstave Calendar, by I. Gillberg, 1755

In fact, the Runes remained in favor among the common people, especially in Sweden. An indication of their enduring popularity is evident from a seventeenth-century inscription on the choir wall of a church in Öland: "The pastor of the parish should know how to read runes and write them." Among the country people of Dalarna, a remote region of western Sweden, survival of knowledge of the Runes has continued into the twentieth century. In Norway, among the Lapps of Finnmark in the country's far North, shaman's drums onto which Runes have been painted are still in use today.

11

The Vikings in the New World

Five hundred years before Columbus "discovered" America, Bjorni Herjólfsson, a young Icelandic merchant, became the first European to see the shores of the New World. Much of the evidence for the history of Norse explorations and the attempted colonization of North America is drawn from two sagas, the more primitive *Grænlendinga Saga (The Saga of the Greenlanders)* and *Eirik's Saga*, written a hundred years later. The latter work is the more sophisticated of the two and contains "improvements," including taking the credit for discovering North America away from Bjorni and giving it to Eirík's son, Leif Eiríksson, nicknamed *heppni*, "the Lucky," for the success of his exploits.

Bjorni found America by accident while on his way to Greenland in the summer of 985 or 986. According to *The Saga of the Greenlanders:*

> The crew asked him if he wanted to land there or not; Bjorni replied, "I think we should sail in close." They did so, and soon they could see that the country was not mountainous, but was well wooded and with low hills. So they put to sea again.*

Around 990, possibly because of the old Norse saying that "the ship knows the way," Leif the Lucky purchased Bjorni's ship and set off with a crew of thirty-five to ex-

*Magnusson, Magnus, *Viking Expansion Westward* (London: The Bodley Head, 1973), p. 127.

plore the unknown lands. He went ashore on Baffin Island which, because he found it rocky and barren, he named *Helluland* (Slab-Land). He went ashore again on Labrador which, being flat and wooded, he named *Markland* (Forest-Land). Two days further sail and they sighted land again. As recorded in *Eirík's Saga:*

> They went ashore and looked about them. The weather was fine. There was dew on the grass, and the first thing they did was to get some of it on their hands and put it to their lips, and to them it seemed the sweetest thing they had ever tasted . . . There was no lack of salmon in the river or the lake, bigger salmon than they had ever seen. The country seemed to them so kind that no winter fodder would be needed for livestock: there was never any frost all winter and the grass hardly withered at all.*

They decided to spend the winter. While exploring the surrounding country, a crew member, a German called Tyrkir, found vines and grapes growing wild. In the spring, when Leif and his crew sailed away, they carried a cargo of timber and dried grapes. Leif named the country *Vínland,* Wineland. To this day, some Americans celebrate Leif Erickson Day on October ninth—three days before Columbus Day. Thanks to the efforts of the late Icelandic historian Prof. Jón Jóhannesson, there is a movement to reinstate Bjorni Herjólfsson as the first European to discover Amer-

*Magnusson, Magnus, *Viking Expansion Westward* (London: The Bodley Head, 1973), p. 128.

ica. We lack only a date and holiday to commemorate Bjorni Herjólfsson Day.

The *Saga of the Greenlanders* relates that another expedition, mounted at great expense by a rich merchant, Thorfinn Karsefni, returned to Vinland probably around the year 1010. The party remained for three years. During that time a child was born to Thorfinn's wife, Guthrith. Their son, Snorri Thorfinnsson, was the first white child recorded as having been born in North America.

At first, the Norsemen traded amicably with the native peoples, whom, however, they contemptuously referred to as *Skrælings* or "Wretches." Before long they began to cheat the Skrælings and soon found themselves in danger. After the third winter, Thorfinn and his party gave up their efforts to colonize the new land and returned to Greenland with a valuable cargo, having established the unfortunate pattern for future trade relations between Europeans and the North American native peoples.

Where then is Leif and Bjorni's Vineland? Norwegian explorer Helge Ingstad and his wife Anne Stine have excavated a site at L'Anse aux Meadows, on the northeastern tip of Newfoundland, a short distance from Épaves Bay. For seven seasons Ingstad and Stine worked the dig, uncovering a complex of ruined buildings that were clearly Norse. Two finds in particular confirmed the origins of the site: a steatite spindle-whorl and a ring-headed bronze pin, both indisputably Norse in origin, probably from the tenth century.

And yet the site at L'Anse aux Meadows cannot have been the *Vinland* of the sagas. No grass for livestock. No salmon rivers. No wild grapes. Moreover, as Magnus Mag-

nusson reminds us, wild grapes have never grown farther North than Passamaquoddy Bay, between Maine and New Brunswick. He concludes: "Most scholars believe, on balance, that the Vínland of the sagas was an area as yet undefined somewhere in the region of New England."*

*Magnusson, Magnus, *Viking Expansion Westward* (London: The Bodley Head, Ltd., 1973), p. 140.

The Rune Carvers of Vineland

Intrepid explorers, the Icelanders were the first Europeans to discover and settle Greenland. From there they explored Baffin Island, Labrador, Newfoundland and ultimately penetrated the North American continent. The questions remaining unanswered to this day are: How deeply did they penetrate, and what marks did they leave?

The colony established in Greenland by Eirík the Red—he named the place Greenland on the theory that people would be more tempted to go there if it had an attractive name—endured for five hundred years at the edge of the known world and then vanished completely from history, probably as a result of climatic changes.

Greenland was a source of great riches for the Norsemen. There were walrus hides for ships' rigging and falcons and polar bears for the European courts. Trappers journeyed far to the North after walrus ivory and furs. A runic inscription from the early fourteenth century, found in a cairn on the island of Kingigtorssuaq (latitude 72 degrees, longitude 55 degrees), testifies to the explorers' habit of recording their exploits, in runic script, at least as late as the 1300s.

Beyond Greenland, the story becomes fascinating and mysterious. The traces left by the Viking explorers are obscure and minimal, and the alleged evidence of their passage is swaddled in controversy. To date, the site at L'Anse aux Meadows stands as the last outpost of scholarly agreement.

Nothing is recorded in the sagas about the presence of Rune carvers in Vineland. There is, however, reason to assume that among the colonizing parties there were those who were conversant with the Runes and knew how to write them. Therefore, without attempting to validate or judge the available evidence, it seems appropriate to enumerate at least a portion of it.

The artifacts in question, all of them either ignored or disputed by scholars, have been found widely scattered across the United States from Spirit Pond in Maine to Rushville, Ohio, and even at several sites in Oklahoma. Then, too, there is the Newport Tower, in Newport, Rhode Island, dismissed by Magnus Magnusson as "the oldest of the Viking red-herrings." But by far the most celebrated of the contested runic finds in North America is the so-called Kensington Rune Stone.

Named for the town of Kensington in Douglas County, Minnesota, near which it was found in the fall of 1898, the stone measures thirty-one inches long, sixteen inches wide and six inches thick, weighs in at over two hundred pounds and has, by now, probably generated its weight in printed scholarly denial.

Kensington Rune Stone

The discoverer of the stone, a Swedish farmer named Olaf Ohman, was clearing trees and pulling stumps on his land when he found a flat slab of stone locked into the roots of an aspen tree. The scornful accusations of fraud with which his find was met so disgusted Ohman that he finally set the stone, fortunately face down, as a granary doorstep.

For almost seven decades after its discovery, the stone—which is currently on display in a museum in Alexandria, Minnesota—was denounced as a hoax. Eric Walgren, formerly a professor at the University of Wisconsin, settled the matter once and for all in his book, *The Kensington Rune Stone: A Mystery Solved* (Madison: University of Wisconsin Press, 1958). The Kensington Rune Stone, according to Walgren, was a hoax. He based his conclusions on lexical distortions and anomalies.

Those of Scandinavian descent living in Minnesota who have viewed the Kensington carving have strong feelings about its authenticity. It is a beautiful artifact and was carved with care by someone. The story on the stone tells of a Norse expedition surprised by Indians. Ten of their number were slaughtered. The date given is 1362. Here is the text:

> *8 Goths and 22 Norsemen on an exploration-tour from Vinland of West. We had camp on two skerries one day's journey North from this stone. We were and fished one day. After we came home found 10 men red of blood and dead.* A(ve) V(irgo) M(aria) *Save from ill. Have 10 men at sea to look after our ship 14 day's journey from this island. Year 1362.*

What were the Norsemen doing in Minnesota in the fourteenth century? At the very least, the idea fires the imagination. From settlements in Newfoundland, Viking exploration undoubtedly included Hudson's Bay, into whose southwest corner the Nelson River debouches. The Norsemen could well have descended the Nelson as far as Lake Winnipeg, traversed the length of the lake and then navigated the Red River down to a point where it is joined by the Otter Tail or Bois de Sioux. Such a journey would have placed the expedition within easy reach of the site of the Kensington Stone.

Runic hoaxes have been found in Illinois and in Missouri. On occasion, Iberic inscriptions are mistaken for runic. And yet, there is a good possibility that the Norsemen did journey out from their Vineland into the North American continent.

Less open to ridicule are the three so-called Spirit Pond Stones, discovered in June of 1971 by Walter Elliott of Quincy, Massachusetts, near Spirit Pond, below the mouth of the Kennebec River in southern Maine. The stone designated as Spirit Pond Number One shows a rude map of the area south of the estuary of the Kennebec River and carries among its inscriptions the runic glyphs for *VINLANT* and the date *1011*. The other two Spirit Pond Stones carry long inscriptions in Runes which have not, to date, been deciphered. There exists one other find from Spirit Pond. It is not well known because the owner keeps it in a bank vault. Donal Buchanan reports that the stone shows "the runic letters *VIN,* some ogham-like marks and a Celtic cross."

It is impossible to carbon date a stone. Yet there is a new method now being tried with certain inscriptions and involving their patina. Gifted amateurs such as Dr. Barry Fell and Dr. Richard Nielson are making forays into the field. We now know that the Vikings were in North America long before the coming of Columbus. The lack of authentication for these runic inscriptions will not change that.

Bind Runes

This intriguing aspect of runology is worthy of a chapter in itself, but a brief introduction will have to suffice. The bind Rune, from the Old Norse *bandrún,* was produced by combining two or more individual Runes into a single figure or glyph, a runic shorthand of sorts. The idea was to create a talisman which combined the power of individual Runes into a unified field of force, usually for a specific purpose, such as protection from ill-health or physical attack or for success in a venture. The bind Runes could be carved into objects—a cup, a sword, a shield—or worn as amulets.

The creation of such talismans or *bandrúnar* was undoubtedly intended to provide a magical link between the Runes. One of the most ancient bind Runes is ᚷ, linking ᚷ and ᚠ. The resulting bind Rune stands for the magical formula *gibu auja,* "give good luck," and is often found carved on ritual weapons. As is evident, the bind Rune takes up less space than a full inscription, where space was always a consideration. Moreover, by employing the ideographic essence of the Rune, a simplicity is achieved that is usually quite pleasing esthetically. In contemporary terms, there is also a conservation of energy which produces a glyph with its own peculiar vibration.

In *Futhark: A Handbook of Rune Magic,* Edred Thorsson offers the following example:

> The purely ideographic bind runes are the most useful in tine magic, and their multiplicity of levels

makes them effective in refined operations of magic. One of the oldest examples of this is found on the brooch of Soest, circa 600–650 C.E.

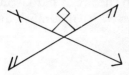

This is formed from the runes ᛉ , ᛁ , ↑ , ᚷ , and ᚠ twice. . . . This *galdrastafr* is a love talisman carved on a broach and then given to a woman. The power of the *taufr* draws upon Odhinic force ᚠ ᚠ , with justice and a call for success ↑ , out of need ᛁ (note the sexual symbolism here), for marriage (erotic union) ᚷ , according to ancestral principles and territory ᛉ .*

Related to the formation of bind Runes is the medieval Germanic tradition of house marks, symbolic monograms or identification marks inscribed onto buildings owned both by the nobility and freemen. Thorsson cites one such house mark

which incorporates the two thorns of life ᚦ and death ᛤ with Thor's hammer between them, and produces the

---

*Thorsson, Edred. *Futhark: A Handbook of Rune Magic* (York Beach, Maine: Samuel Weizer, 1984), p. 101.

esoteric reading "Between life and death may my estate increase and prosper."*

Another expression of linked (as opposed to bound) Runes is found in the art of old Germanic architecture in the forms of *Fachwerk* (half-timbered) building style. As

Thorsson writes:

> Originally, the timbers of the *Fachwerk* were placed in such a way as to form the shape of a rune. The magical significance of this is that the runic power would then be imparted to the building and its inhabitants. This custom continued on into the days when the builders no longer knew why the timbers were laid in these particular ways—it be-

*Ibid., p. 10.

came simple tradition. The now familiar "Dutch hex signs" also are ultimately derived from a runic source.*

This half-timbered building style can be seen throughout northern Europe. It is common in the Tudor architecture of England, and is to be found wherever exposed beams make up part of the architectural statement, including the up-market "Tudor" homes of Greenwich, Connecticut and Beverly Hills, California.

The Runes in Contemporary Culture

In English literature, there are references to the Runes in one of the odes of William Collins, in the work of Horace Walpole, Matthew Arnold and Thomas Hardy. M. R. James's classic ghost story "Casting the Runes" was published in 1911. J. R. R. Tolkien invented his own Runes for *The Lord of the Rings.* A recent resurgence of interest in the Runes has resulted in the publication of a number of books on runecraft in England, Italy, Germany and the United States. Even novelist Ursula Le Guin has added Runes to her mix. One of the main characters in Alice Walker's 1989 novel, *The Temple of My Familiar,* is called "Suwelo" *(Sowelu),* a name whose meaning is given as "the rune of wholeness."

Runic themes are also represented in contemporary music with such works as the ballet score *Runes—Solara March,* music by Keith Jarrett and choreography by Alvin Ailey, and the albums *Runes* by Kano and *Wunjo* by Giles

*Ibid., p. 7.

Reaves. Runes decorate the album cover for Jethro Tull's *Broadsword and the Beast.* Led Zeppelin recorded a song called "The Battle of Evermore" in which occur the lines:

> *The Magic Runes are writ in gold*
> *To bring the balance back.*

This album, *Led Zeppelin IV,* is referred to as the "Runes Album."

Paintings and sculptures are now being produced by at least a dozen artists who are incorporating runic glyphs into their work. In addition, there is a growing cottage industry in things runic from hand-crafted jewelry to fabrics to beautifully carved sets of Rune stones.

Finally, the Runes are beginning to serve in a new role as film artifacts. In Terry Jones's *Eric the Viking,* Eartha Kitt portrays a shaman who casts the Runes. In a Blake Edwards film, *Skin Deep,* a woman is shown searching in the burnt-out remains of her house for her Runes. And so it goes.

Any Oracle is a reflection of the culture in which it evolves. In the Runes, we are provided with a symbolic system that derives from an Oracle arising within the forms of Western thought. Whether in English villages, among the Lapp shamans of northern Norway, or in rituals practiced by small bands of chanting Odinists from Iceland to Austin, Texas—the Runes remain, threaded back to their antiquity while finding new uses and applications in our contemporary culture.

It is both timely and providential that the Viking Runes once again be restored to service as a Western Oracle.

THE TRAVELLER'S PRAYER

The life of God surrounds me.
The love of God enfolds me.
The power of God protects me.
The presence of God watches over me.
Wherever I am, God is.
And wherever God is, all is well.

—Unity

Bronze Buddha from northern India, brought to Sweden during
the Migration Period, circa 600 A.D.

2

CONSULTING THE ORACLE

Our lives are ordered for us by the Divine so that nothing is too much.
We are never given more than we can handle; but nothing is too loose,
either. We can always breathe, yes, but at times the water is up to where
the wings of the nose barely touch. And as we grow? As we grow, the
water rises. Still we are preserved from drowning. And that is providen-
tial, because our nature needs a situation that reminds it: You are always
at the beginning. In the life of the Spirit, you are always at the beginning.

—Dr. Allan W. Anderson

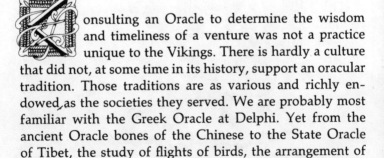onsulting an Oracle to determine the wisdom and timeliness of a venture was not a practice unique to the Vikings. There is hardly a culture that did not, at some time in its history, support an oracular tradition. Those traditions are as various and richly en-dowed as the societies they served. We are probably most familiar with the Greek Oracle at Delphi. Yet from the ancient Oracle bones of the Chinese to the State Oracle of Tibet, the study of flights of birds, the arrangement of clouds, the patterns formed on water—the diversity of oracular styles is truly remarkable.

In Roman times, using a technique known as *Sortae Ver-*

gilianae, anyone seeking a clue to their future would open the *Aeneid* at random and read the first line on which their eyes fell. For centuries, people in the West wishing to learn the will of the Divine on matters of importance have consulted the Bible in a similar manner.

For a truly Western contemporary oracular system we must, in the end, turn to the Runes.

CONSULTING THE RUNECARDS

You may want to set aside a certain time each day to consult the Oracle. Some people draw a card when they arise in the morning, others before they go to bed. There are those who have a special place where they keep their RuneCards and book, and where they do their readings. Before consulting the RuneCards, you might light a candle or say a prayer, especially if the situation confronting you is a difficult one. My prayer is always the same: *I will to will Thy Will.*

There is a simple meditation exercise I learned from the Buddhist teacher Thich Nhat Hanh which I find very calming. All it requires is a willingness to sit in silence and observe your breathing. As you breathe, think these words:

> *Breathing in, I calm body and mind.*
> *Breathing out, I smile.*

Continue repeating the words to yourself. On each in-breath, *Breathing in, I calm body and mind,* and on each out-breath, the words *Breathing out I smile.* After a while, change the phrase to:

27

(on the in-breath) *Dwelling in the present moment,*
(on the out-breath) *Wonderful moment, only moment.*

Watch your breath, watch the thoughts that come. Release all cares and concerns. A few minutes of repeating each couplet will suffice. This is a simple and effective way of preparing to consult the Knowing Self.*

Focus is important. But if the ordinary business of living intrudes, you can always consult the Runes without formal preparation. Your need is what brings the Runes into play. And remember, you *are* in the realm of play, sacred play. A particularly good time to consult the Runes is when you have exhausted your own resources and are facing a situation about which you possess limited or incomplete information. Focus the issue clearly in your mind, shuffle the deck, then draw a RuneCard.

When you draw a card for someone else, ask the person to formulate the matter of concern clearly in their mind but *not* state it aloud. This eliminates any unconscious personal bias in your interpretation of the Runes.

If a friend who is not with you could benefit from the perspective of a Rune reading, the telephone is your ally: Ask your friend to think of an issue, then draw a card from your deck. Consulting the RuneCards across a continent is as effective as sitting face to face with your friend.

---

*Throughout this book, the term *self* is used to represent the ego-self, and *Self* to signify the Higher Self, the Divine Within. Ego disorders abound, but they can be set to rights. The ego does not require beating into submission, but rather a more conscious understanding of the quality of power represented in its proper relationship to the Divine Self. A harmonious relationship between the Self and the self is a function *not* of "power over" but of being "in partnership with."

APPROPRIATE ISSUES

An appropriate issue *is anything that relates to timeliness and right action.* Notice that the word *issue* is used rather than *question.* A question would be, "Should I end this relationship?" To state it as an issue, you would say, "The issue is my relationship." This small distinction is crucial. If you ask a question and the Oracle provides the answer, then your role is a passive one. However, if you present an issue, and the Oracle comments on that issue, it is up to you to determine for yourself what constitutes right action.

If you don't have a specific issue in mind, and still you feel drawn to consult the RuneCards, simply ask: *What do I need to know for my life now?* The Oracle's reply will always be instructive.

UPRIGHT AND REVERSED READINGS

Nine of the RuneCards read the same regardless of how you draw them. So even if you draw one of the nine with its name and number upside-down, remember that the glyph reads the same however you draw the card.

The other sixteen can be read in two ways—either Upright or Reversed. When you turn to the interpretations at the back of the book, you will find an Upright and a Reversed reading for each of the sixteen cards.

A word of explanation is called for concerning the first card, *Mannaz, The Self.* When the card is drawn Upright, the image of the glyph *appears* Reversed, reflected on the water ᛗ , as if to say, it is by reflection—self-reflection and the ways in which others see us—that we come to know ourselves. So despite the reversed image: *If the legend "*I. THE SELF*" is at the bottom, the card is Upright.*

Be mindful that reversal is always contained within *The Self,* even when it is drawn Upright. How like the self! In fact, regardless of how you draw this card, it is always advisable to read *both* the Upright and Reversed interpretations.

It is well to remember that the appearance of a Reversed RuneCard is not a cause for alarm but rather an indication that care and attention are required for your conduct to be correct. Whether you draw your RuneCard Upright or Reversed, you may see fit to read *both* aspects; to do so will keep you in touch with the unseen side of the situation—that which is not presently being expressed.

RUNIC OVERRIDE

Occasionally you may find that the counsel you receive doesn't seem to apply to the issue posed. When this occurs, consider the possibility that your unconscious has tuned in to a more significant issue, something you are avoiding, or something of which you are not immediately aware. This *Runic Override* serves as an automatic fail-safe device. Similarly, if you find yourself caught between two issues and can't decide which one to address, the Runes will select for you by speaking to the issue of most immediate concern.

YES/NO ANSWERS

Although I find myself saying it often, it bears repeating that the Runes do not provide answers. To give someone an answer, my grandfather used to say, robs them forever of acquiring that answer for themselves. And yet, having made this point, I want to offer an exception to the rule.

Over the years, I have frequently found myself in situations where I needed to make a decision immediately. No time to think things out. No opportunity to obtain more information. Simply, the telephone rings: "Will you or won't you?" "Yes or no?" So I devised a technique for getting myself off "stuck."

Draw a single RuneCard. If the glyph is Upright, then the answer is "Yes." If Reversed, the answer is "No." If you happen to draw one of the Runes which reads the same Upright and Reversed, draw again.

Another variant of this technique is to toss the Rune-Cards in the air. If the majority fall face up, the answer is "Yes." If more cards land face down, the answer is "No."

Remember, this technique is not meant to be used when examining issues of substance. It can be very helpful at moments when what you do or don't do matters less than simply getting on with your life.

KEEPING A RUNE JOURNAL

As you establish your practice of working with the RuneCards, you may find it helpful to record your insights in a journal by marking down the particular cards you draw, then writing your own brief interpretation. Note the time, date and the prevailing conditions in your life at the moment. Recording these readings in your Rune Journal will help you to become more familiar with the Runes and their symbolism and, over time, will enable you to judge for yourself the relevance and accuracy of the Oracle as a guide to self-change.

CONSULTING TWO ORACLES

Using the RuneCards interchangeably with the Rune stones as I do, at different times I find myself drawn to one form of the Oracle or the other. I like the solidity and weight of the stones and it pleases me to dip into the bag. At the same time, the RuneCards fit easily into my pocket and can go anywhere without calling attention to themselves. Moreover, because the cards are so visually evocative, people report that their intuitive knowing is often stimulated directly by the images without their having to turn to the interpretations in the book.

When I first began working with the Runes, in order to confirm their responses with those of a known and wise friend, I would often address the same issue both to the *I Ching** and to the Runes. Time after time, I found the two

The I Ching or Book of Changes, Bollingen Edition (Princeton: Princeton University Press, 1977).

Oracles to be in accord, sometimes identical in their symbolic content, always a mutual enrichment.

These days, I occasionally consult both the RuneCards and the stones on the same issue. I find that a dialogue between the stones and the RuneCards often provides me with an additional dimension of understanding.

Each form of the Oracle has a style and a character which is unique. And each has its own message to impart.

SHUFFLING THE RUNECARDS

Shuffling or mixing the RuneCards while you are formulating your issue is itself a kind of meditation. Because the deck contains only twenty-five cards, and because of the thickness of the cards, conventional shuffling is less effective than simply mixing the cards to change their order. So take your time, pausing now and then to turn half the deck in the opposite direction, so that the order of Upright and Reversed cards is also varied. When you are finished mixing, you may choose to take half the deck and give it a final twist, once again changing the direction of Upright and Reversed cards.

Twittering of the Birds

This technique, said to be Chinese in origin, calls for spreading the RuneCards out in front of you on a flat surface and stirring or moving them around with your fingers. As your fingers touch every card, and as you review your issue in your mind, a subtle connection is created with the Oracle. *Twittering of the Birds* can be another pleasing form of meditation.

TOSSED SALAD

This technique was born at a time when I was at my wit's end. In a moment of terminal frustration, I tossed the entire deck in the air. The cards all landed face-down except for three: *Flow, The Unknowable* and *Harvest.* The message seemed clear: *Just start things flowing and trust the Will of Heaven; what is yours will come to you in its season.*

There will be times when you use this technique that no card shows its image. When that happens, collect the cards and toss again. If more than three cards fall face-up, you have two choices. You can collect those that fall face-up and keep tossing them until three or less images are showing. Then read those Runes. Or, if your issue is complex, you may choose to read *all* the upturned cards, deriving an extended message from their interpretations.

SINGLE-CARD DRAW

Drawing a single RuneCard is the simplest and, often, the most effective use of the Oracle. Any time you need an overview of a situation, in moments of crisis, or when you lack sufficient information to decide what constitutes right action, the *Single-Card Draw* will help you to focus more clearly on your issue and provide you with a fresh perspective.

Many people find that drawing a single daily Rune, or *Rune of Right Action,* gives them an indication of what kind of day to expect. As one veteran Rune caster put it, "If I'm in for heavy weather, I can put on my long johns before going out in the storm."

Drawing a card each day is an ideal way for someone new to the Runes to learn their meanings effortlessly. You are, so to speak, studying a Rune a day—familiarizing yourself with the interpretations, coming to terms with Reversed readings as natural phases of your own cycle, learning to watch for patterns in the way the same Runes come up time and again during certain periods in your life.

If you have had a particularly trying or exhilarating day, you may wish to draw a RuneCard again in the evening for an evaluation of how you've conducted yourself.

THREE-CARD SPREAD

When a situation arises that calls for more in-depth consideration, the *Three-Card Spread* can be most helpful. The three RuneCards stand for *The Overview, The Challenge,* and *The Course of Action Called For.* With an issue clearly in mind, mix the cards, then divide them into three stacks. Next, turn over the top card of each stack and read the cards from right to left.

A Sample Reading

During the twenty years Beth has been living in Los Angeles, she has watched the air quality go from bad to worse, freeway traffic turn into gridlock, and the cost of living skyrocket. At work she found herself yearning for clear mountain streams but feared that she wouldn't be able to make a living away from the city. Then one day an old friend living in Boulder invited Beth to come to Colorado and share her house. Wondering if this was the opportunity she had been dreaming of, Beth decided to consult the Runes. Using the *Three-Card Spread,* these are the cards she drew:

3. Course of Action	2. Challenge	1. Overview
ㄱ	⋈	⟨

6. Initiation Reversed   *22. Breakthrough*   *13. Harvest*

The fact that she had drawn *Harvest,* "a Rune of beneficial outcomes" as the Overview of the Situation, excited Beth. *Breakthrough,* in the Challenge position, told her to risk it, "to leap empty-handed into the void." However, *Initiation Reversed* concerning *The Course of Action Called For,* gave her an anxious moment until she read, "the old way has come to an end: You simply cannot repeat the old and not suffer." She decided to give notice at her job the next day.

However, in the morning before leaving for work, she reread the three interpretations and saw their message in a new light. "The harvest promised *isn't* immediate," she told me. "A span of time is involved. And yes, transformation is the Challenge, but there's a warning about taking hasty action and collapsing myself into the future—which is exactly what I intended to do. And *Initiation Reversed* calls for patience, constancy, and perseverance. Meaning, if I'm going to make the move, do it right."

Reading the interpretations a second time helped Beth to see clearly that, although she really wanted to leave Los Angeles, she needed to make her plans in a careful and well-thought-out way. She decided to spend two weeks with her friend in Boulder, research job possibilities, and see what Colorado life was like for a single woman.

Beth's experience with the RuneCards is a useful example of how your desires can bias your reading of the interpretations. When the issue is one of major life change, a second reading by dawn's cool light can show you another perspective.

FIVE-CARD SPREAD

The *Five-Card Spread* adds two new elements: *The Sacrifice* and *New Situation Evolving*. Sacrifice, as used here, refers to that which must be peeled away, shed, discarded in order for new conditions to develop. The New Situation Evolving will give you an indication of what you can expect after you have attended to the first four steps.

When I use the Rune stones for a Three- or Five-Rune Spread, I usually replace one stone before drawing the next, so that all twenty-five stones are available to provide a commentary on my issue. However, when I lay out a spread with five Runecards, in making the selection I almost always read the cards in the sequence in which they appear.

Begin by clearly formulating your issue in your mind. Shuffle or mix your deck, then cut the cards, placing the cut portion face-up on the remainder of the deck. Rather than reshuffling and drawing a card four more times, let the top card provide the commentary for the *Overview*. Let the card beneath it represent the *Challenge,* and so on, until you have drawn five cards to comment on:

1: *Overview of the Situation*
2: *Nature of the Challenge*
3: *Course of Action Called For*
4: *Sacrifice Required*
5: *New Situation Evolving*

After undertaking the Five-Card Spread, you may see fit to draw one more card, the *Rune of Summation,* to get the gist or essence of the entire reading. I have found this a very helpful technique.

MAKING BIND RUNES

This practice, deriving as it does from the ancient Germanic and Nordic practice of combining two or more Runes into a single unit (see pp. 20–21), had a clearly magical purpose in the Viking period. In our time, however, whenever you need to focus your energy on a task, or desire to achieve a certain outcome, making a bind Rune can serve as an aid to memory, a talisman of intention.

In Umberto Eco's novel, *Foucault's Pendulum,* there is an extraordinary example of the use of a bind Rune to embrace the sacred sites of the Medieval World in a single configuration:

> If you take a map of Europe and Asia and trace the development of the plan beginning with the castle in the north and moving from there to Jerusalem, from Jerusalem to Agarttha, from Agarttha to Chartres, from Chartres to the shores of the Mediterranean, and from there to Stonehenge, you will find that you have drawn a rune that looks more or less like this,

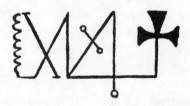

And the same rune, ideally, would connect the main centers of Templar esotericism: Amiens,

Troyes—Saint Bernard's domain at the edge of the Foret d'Orient—Reims, Chartres, Rennes-le-Chateau, and Mont-Saint-Michel, a place of ancient druidic worship. The rune also recalls the constellation of the Virgin.*

Practical Bind Runes

Say you are concerned with right action in a situation where you and several others are competing for a promotion. With the issue in mind, and drawing from the deck, you might receive the following three cards: ⌡ , *Flow Reversed,* ▷ , *Gateway,* and Υ , *Protection.* The bind Rune formed might look like this:

and its meaning might be: *"I will not strive excessively, but will examine my own motives, willing to wait on the Will of Heaven, keeping my emotions under control, secure in the knowledge that I will progress."*

Recently, I made a bind Rune for two friends who have been in a relationship for some time. Lately, one of them has been feeling blocked, not growing at the same rate as the other. A restoration of balance was what seemed to be called for. I drew two cards and got ⌡ , *Warrior Reversed,* and ß , *Growth.* The order in which the cards were drawn—with *Growth* second—seemed encouraging. The interpretation might be: *"Lost energy can be replaced by finding a new way to relate to one another; by honoring the conditions for new growth, the blossom-*

*Umberto Eco, *Foucault's Pendulum* (New York: Harcourt Brace Jovanovich, 1989).

ing can occur." Here, with the *Warrior* Rune set Upright, is the bind Rune:

You might then draw your bind Rune on a bit of paper and keep it in your pocket. Or you might place it on your desk or some place where you will see it throughout the day. The couple in question had a silversmith incise their bind Rune on a silver medallion. You will discover your own way of utilizing your bind Runes.

While it is difficult to combine more than five or six Runes in one figure, my friend Tad Mann designed a bind Rune which holds in its architecture all twenty-four Runes of the original futhark alphabet.

As it is my abiding intention to work with the Runes in a non-magical context, and given the original magical purpose of bind Runes, I consulted the Oracle concerning the appropriateness of including this exercise. I stated the issue in this way: *How can the bind Runes serve us in furthering the work of self-change and personal growth in keeping with the Will of the Divine?* I drew , the Rune of *Harvest,* with its reminder that in consulting the Runes on any issue the ultimate purpose is "the harvest of the self."

ONE PERSON'S PRACTICE

Over the years, I have received a great many insightful letters telling of the ways different people consult the Oracle. My intention was to select passages from a variety of those letters to include here. The letter which follows, however, provides such a succinct and accessible description of many people's practice with the Runes that it seems sufficient in itself.

In 1984, while I and my family were living in Khartoum in the Sudan, on a whim I ordered and received a copy of your *Book of Runes.*

At the time, I laid the stones infrequently, and found that although they gave me food for thought, I seemed to be missing something essential. Fortunately, I recorded the castings in a makeshift journal: scraps and bits of paper grabbed at odd moments, but still dated, interpreted and with some personal observations noted.

My life has changed radically since that time and now, with the clarity of hindsight, when I read my journal—my own notes and thoughts—I see that my castings foretold where I was headed. They gave me a very accurate reading of my frame of mind, even though I had *no* understanding at the time!

These days I cast on a regular basis—about every three weeks, although in times of stress, I might turn to the Runes twice a week. I've learned to read them a little differently now. I pay attention to what catches my fancy in the interpretation, and muse on what that phrase or sentence means to the most inner me—at *this* moment.

I no longer worry or wonder if I'm "getting it" or not. I try to listen to the words that catch my eye, for it's *me* calling my own self to attention.

Re-reading my journal, you might suspect the Runes *foretold.* But it wasn't the Runes—it was *me* all along. I just didn't know how to listen before. At least not to me.

Reading the Runes seems to give a clarity to my life by reminding me to slow down and pay attention to what I'm doing. I don't just react or, worse, block out what is going on. I *think* about what's bothering me and try to come up with a number of solutions. I now *confront.* It's a very good feeling.

Each of you will go through different phases in your relationship to the Oracle as a self-counseling tool. There will be times when you use the RuneCards daily, other times when you use them not at all. The Runes have proven themselves to be a trustworthy witness, a good companion for those who have chosen self-change as their path. When you find yourself at a crossroads or when you are faced with an issue of right action and you desire to act for the highest good of all concerned, the Oracle is there to serve you.

THE PEACE OF WILD THINGS

When despair for the world grows in me
and I wake in the night at the least sound
in fear of what my life and my children's lives may be,
I go and lie down where the wood drake rests
in his beauty on the water, and the great heron feeds.
I come into the peace of wild things
who do not take their lives with forethought of grief.
I come into the presence of still water.
And I feel above me the day-blind stars
waiting with their light. For a time
I rest in the grace of the world, and am free.

—Wendell Berry

3

RUNECARD GAMES, SACRED & ORDINARY

Have I not here the best cards for the game. . . .

—William Shakespeare, *King John*

*Leading an authentic life has to do with being true to archetypal patterns
that are expressions of the Self. When this is so, what we do has a sacred
dimension and gives us a sense of meaning.*

—Jean Shinoda Bolen

he essence of this volume's subtitle, *Sacred Play for
Self-Discovery,* could be expressed in another way:
*It is by recognizing the play of the sacred in our lives that
we discover the true nature of the self.* From our earliest years, we
learn by playing. It is the element of play in a culture that
preserves tradition and fosters the wisdom that transcends
fashion. Creating a ceremony or sacred game allows us to
experience a *true present* and, at the same time, acknowledges
our sense of community.

I have been creating and collecting Rune games for some
years now. The seven games included in this chapter range

from the sacred to the ordinary. They can be played equally well with RuneCards or with the stones.

LETTERS TO YOURSELF

The inspiration for *Letters to Yourself* comes from a nineteenth-century learning technique used to teach young children to read. I still have one of the old-time primers called *Farmer Brown's Farm.* The first chapter begins as follows:

This is a 🌾 . He has a 🐄 and two 🐷 . This is his 🏠 . There is a 🚜 in the yard. . . .

As a child, I spent considerable time with *Farmer Brown's Farm.* It made reading much more fun than the "Spot is a dog. See Spot run" approach to literacy.

Letters is a game you can play by yourself. While you mix the RuneCards, be thinking of the ways in which some situation might evolve. It is best if you haven't any idea what the outcome will be—or even what you would like to happen.

Begin by making an opening statement or posing an opening question, and then pick a RuneCard. The card you select will respond to your statement or address your question. Replace each card in the deck after you draw. Continue playing until the Runes have helped to clarify your thinking. Here is an example:

"I am planning a trip to India. If I carry out my plans, I can expect—" I drew ↑, *Flow. Laguz may call you to study spiritual matters,* the interpretation told me, which is, indeed, the purpose of my journey. "The man I am going to meet in India will help me—" I drew ß, *Growth.* I noted, in particular, the passage about growth in *one's relationship to one's Self or to the Divine.* "What troubles me is that I will be out of touch with home for three weeks. What is the Oracle's advice?" I drew ⋈, *Breakthrough* which reassured me, saying, *Because the timing is right, the outcome is assured although not, from the present vantage point, predictable. . . .* I interpreted the message of the three RuneCards to be: "Carry out your plans, all will be well."

As you can see, this game can continue as long as any uncertainty remains, or as long as you have questions. Notice, the question is not put in a form that would require a "Yes" or "No" answer. Rather, you are asking the Runes to comment on your situation.

If two people are concerned over the same issue, then you can alternate statements or questions. I have played this game often over the years and have always found it helpful.

Since this exercise is in letter form, you might choose to write down your statements or questions, then record the Runes you select. In that way, you will create your own "primer" for conduct.

MIRRORS

Mirrors was suggested by Indian Poker, a card game we used to play as children. The assumption of *Mirrors* is that the RuneCard you draw has a message for you, something useful to say concerning your life. It may be information of which you are fully aware but have resisted recognizing. It may be a clue to resolving a dilemma. Or it may simply be a message from your unconscious which you need to hear.

It is best for each player to have their own deck of Rune-Cards, though that is not essential. The game is richest when played by people who know one another fairly well.

Say that two of you decide to play. Each person chooses a RuneCard and, as in Indian Poker, without looking at it, holds the card to their forehead with the image facing out so that the other player can see it. Begin by closing your eyes, taking a deep breath and relaxing. Now see if you can intuit your own card. State whether you believe the glyph is Upright or Reversed. If you guess correctly, look up the card and comment on how the reading applies to your life now.

If you guess incorrectly, ask the other player for the first clue. Ask for as many clues as it takes for you to identify your card. The other player must answer honestly but, at the same time, try not to give away your card by the clues.

At first glance, you might think that this game is only for people already conversant with the Runes and their inter-pretations. And to be sure, you will find yourself going to the interpretations for the substance of your clues. *Mirrors* is a playful way to learn the meaning of each RuneCard. And as you try to guess the Rune behind the clue, your mind will be recalling what you know of the text.

For instance, if someone gave you this clue, "You could make a beginning by cleaning out your closet," would you have an idea which RuneCard you were holding against your forehead? You might think about separating yourself from the unnecessary things you've held on to from the past and guess *Separation.* Close but not the card.

Another clue might be, "Completing this project is the most important challenge facing you right now." And because it talks about "terminations and new beginnings," you might guess your card was *Strength.* Wrong again.

The next clue could be, "When you finally do complete this project, you'll feel as though you've given birth." You might recall the passage that goes, *Now it is time to enter the delivery room . . .* and still not be able to picture the glyph.

One final clue from the interpretation would be: The completion of beginnings is what *blank* requires. What *Inguz* requires. So you're holding the eighth card, *Fertility,* New Beginnings. Now read the complete interpretation and see how it applies to your life.

Mirrors can help to familiarize you with the interpretations for the RuneCards and, at the same time, provide you with unexpected communications from your unconscious. In addition, the game offers a nonthreatening and playful way to learn how others see you.

TALKING WITH THE GRANDPARENTS

The idea for Talking with the Grandmothers and the Grandfathers comes from the Native American Indian ritual ways that are presently inspiring many people in our culture. The Grandfathers show us how to go through the world, how to strengthen our Warrior nature, yet still follow what Black Elk calls the path with a heart. The Grandmothers are the Wise Women whose knowledge guides us through our illnesses, our celebrations, our births and our deaths.

When a child has no grandparents from whom to hear the old stories and inhale the old ways; when, as we follow the path of the Spiritual Warrior, we yearn to sit in council with the Wise Old Ones; when we are gnarled and old ourselves, and there is no one left to join us beside the fire and share what we know to be true—then it is time to talk with the Grandfathers.

When our creative flow has dried up; when we require a ceremony for the celebration of life; when we are feeling empty and long to be nurtured; when we are mourning and in need of consolation—let us invoke the Grandmothers.

Sample Questions

"Grandfather, all my life I have struggled to know my path. I am weary and my life does not satisfy me. What advice do you have for me?"

"Grandmother, my mother is dying, please comfort me."

"Grandfather, marriage is a commitment that frightens me. What can you tell me from your experience to help me meet with courage the challenges that lie ahead?"

"Grandmother, now that I am a grandparent myself, what is the gift that I have to give this new generation?"

You may want to draw more than one card in order to hear fully the wisdom of the Old Ones. If so, you might use the *Three-Card Spread,* where the three answers represent *Overview, Challenge, Course of Action Called for.* Then again, a single RuneCard may suffice. Feel free to address any question to either the Grandmothers or the Grandfathers.

This game brings ancient wisdom into our lives by putting us in touch with the archetypes of the Grandmothers and the Grandfathers. Honor them with your respect and they will nurture and serve you.

CEREMONY FOR SACRED MARRIAGE

Not long ago, I was given a gift of sacred herbs by two master carvers from the Northwest, Joe David and Loren White. We sat in council together one evening in the hills above Ojai, California, while they explained how to use their gift.

On the night of the day the Japanese buried their emperor, I performed the ceremony. My objective was three-fold: to separate myself from past ways of relating to women; to open myself to meeting a woman who will be a partner for me and the mother of our child; to prepare myself for sacred marriage.

Loren and Joe David had instructed me to perform the ceremony in water in order to place myself symbolically in the presence of the Great Mother. I live on the shore of the Pacific Ocean. So that night, feeling a bit foolish and hoping no one was watching, I carried out the ceremony standing in the surf.

Afterward, I returned to my house, dried off, and sat quietly in front of the fire. First, I said a prayer to the Great Mother. Next, I wrote down five open-ended affirmations to be completed by the Runes. Speaking the words of the first affirmation aloud, I drew a RuneCard. Then I replaced the card in the deck and repeated the procedure four more times. Here are the affirmations and the Runes they evoked:

I have surrendered my old ways, and so I draw ᚢ *(Strength Reversed).*
I await now, without desire, in a state of ᛒ *(Growth Reversed)*
I give thanks and praise for my lot which is ☐ *(The Unknowable)*

I submit to the Will of Heaven which is W *(Movement Reversed)*
I know that the new life will bring X *(Partnership)*

The reading was startling and yet typical of the Runes for both its humor and its bull's-eye marksmanship.

Strength Reversed calls not only for serious thoughts about the quality of my relationship to my Higher Self, but also recommends that I "not draw back from the passage into darkness. When in deep water, become a diver." I had just dived twice into the ocean in the dark!

Growth Reversed deals with "aspects of character that interfere with the growth of new life" and commands me to "Strip away until you can identify the obstacles to growth." Not only had I decided to surrender my old habits, I had also stripped naked before entering the ocean!

Indeed, I was placing my life, my future, in the hands of *The Unknowable.* The commentary for the twenty-fifth Rune says "Relinquishing control is the ultimate challenge for the Spiritual Warrior."

With *Movement Reversed,* I was being told that "The opportunity at hand may be precisely to avoid action." I was asked to remain mindful that "What is yours will come to you."

Finally, I welcomed the future, which, appropriately enough, turned out to be the Rune of *Partnership.* I was reminded that "true partnership is only achieved by separate and whole beings." So be content to wait, the Runes were saying, and while you wait honor your separateness and seek union with your Higher Self, union with the Divine.

I relate this experience to demonstrate how, in matters of serious purpose, you can create ceremony to meet your own needs and the Runes will support your intention.

RUNE PLAY

Do you remember, as a child, sitting in the doctor's office, finding coloring book drawings of a dense, leafy jungle, and being asked in the caption: "How many monkeys can you find hidden in the jungle?" And when you really looked, there they were: monkeys outlined in tree bark, monkeys disguised as vines, monkeys made from the outlines formed between leaves, trunk monkeys, branch monkeys, root monkeys!

Sometimes Runes appear in nature's forms, in tree branches, rock formations, clouds. Just when you are wondering whether or not to call the doctor, a cloud combed by the wind stretches itself into the soft lightning-bolt form of ⚡ , the Rune of *Wholeness.*

Once you begin *Rune Play,* you will discover Runes on license plates and bridge scaffoldings, among graffiti on walls, in cracks in the pavement, in house beams and on road signs. When you really look, you will find Runes everywhere.

Pick a Rune in the morning. Then see if you can find the runic symbol in the twisting branches of a favorite tree. During a meditation or while resting, visualize the Rune on your mental screen. Stand in front of a mirror and form the glyph with your body—a kind of Rune yoga. Try to spot the image in textures, on patterned surfaces. During meetings or while you're daydreaming, draw the image, doodle it. While out driving or walking with your children, invite them into the game. Kids love to pick their own RuneCard, then try and find it in the world around them. Let the last image you hold in your mind before you drift off to sleep be the Rune you picked for the day.

No doubt you can create your own versions of Rune Play to enjoy with others or by yourself.

DYING TIME

Among people who have reported near-death experiences, there are those who tell of another reality so beautiful that they actually feel anger at having to return to the world of the living. They may spend the rest of their lives yearning for that reality. Others, on their return, feel everything more intensely and so savor the joy of each moment. The object of *Dying Time* is to help us live our lives from this realization and with this joy.

Begin by telling yourself that the moment has come for you to die. Enough time remains for you to review your life and consider what you've left undone. Words you wanted to say to someone but never said. Old relationships that went awry where you would gladly make amends. Aspects of your nature that stand in need of transformation.

Take a moment to be still. Focus on your breathing; be aware of how precious each breath has become. Let all thoughts of the daily round depart. They are of no consequence to you now.

Dying Time is a game that can be played using both the RuneCards and the stones. The RuneCards you choose will represent the *Key Elements* of your life, while the Rune stones you draw will stand for the *Blessings* you have derived from those life situations. If you don't have a set of Rune stones, record your Key Element card, return it to the deck, then draw another card for the Blessing.

Take your deck of RuneCards and begin to mix them. As

you do, consider the way you have lived your life, then select one of the following questions:

- What has been most difficult for me?
- What do I do best?
- What or whom do I love most?
- Who is my enemy?

Other questions may occur to you. When you have decided on the first question, choose a RuneCard to comment on your question. If the commentary does not fully satisfy your need, draw a second card.

Next put your hand into the bag of Rune stones and mix them, consciously touching each of the stones while reviewing the progress you have made in resolving this question. Pick a stone and place it on top of your card. Consider the Key Element in the light of the Blessing. Now that you are dying, the time has come to see that there is another side to what you consider your failures, and to recognize the blessings that attend all situations—no matter how well disguised the Blessing may be.

Perhaps *Dying Time* will suggest ways in which you can activate some of the unrealized possibilities of your life.

RUNE PUNS

Over the years, friends and strangers alike seem to have been afflicted with uncontrollable urges to provide me with Rune puns. Weary of being serious, I thought I would share some of these little beauties with you. For a start, take talk show hosts.

> *Host:* "Now that your book's doing well, I suppose you'll improve your living quarters?"
> *Self:* "How do you mean?"
> *Host:* "Get yourself a *Rune with a view!*"

And again:
> *Host:* "Do you live by yourself in Malibu?"
> *Self:* "Yes, I do."
> *Host (breaking up):* "Maybe you'd better get a *Runemate!*"

Or, especially on the predawn and after-midnight circuits:
> *Host:* "Oh! You'll be the *Rune* of me! You'll drive me to *rack and Rune!*

And yet again:
> *Host:* "What do you call someone who's just crazy about the Runes? A *runatic,* I suppose?"

Then there are the runic puns that come out of nowhere. They always take me pleasantly by surprise.

An elderly woman in a Waldenbooks Store in Boston watched sympathetically as I lifted a stack of *The Book of Runes* onto a table at a book signing. She shook her head and clucked in a Down East twang, "Careful, sonny, or you'll get *runatoid arthritis!*"

My favorite rune pun was the work of David Spangler, who, at the start of my first book tour, gave me a baseball on which he had written *"May you always hit homerunes."*

I'm sure you get the point by now. I don't want to Rune the game for you by overdoing it. If you were a talk show host, you might observe that, judging from this last game, it appears my life already is in Runes.

As you become familiar with the RuneCards, no doubt you will create games of your own, games both sacred and ordinary. I hope you will share your game ideas—or any choice Rune Puns—with us.

Bronze Age Rock Carving, Sweden

ELEGY

Do not stand at my grave and weep.
I am not there. I do not sleep.
I am a thousand winds that blow.
I am the diamond's glint on snow.
I am the sunlight on ripened grain.
I am the gentle autumn's rain.
When you awaken in the morning's hush
I am the swift uplifting rush
of quiet birds in circled flight.
I am the soft stars that shine at night.
Do not stand at my grave and cry.
I am not there. I did not die.

—Author Unknown

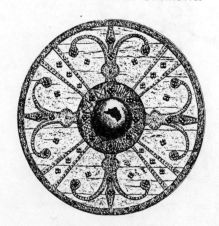

Wooden Rune Shield,
Nedenes Amt, Norway, twelfth century

4

RUNES AND HEALING

And to the centurion Jesus said, "Go thy way; be it done unto thee as thou hast believed." And his servant was healed in the selfsame hour.

—Matthew 8:13

The Runes as described here are healing, merciful Runes; they will do you no harm.

—Martin D. Raynor, Ph.D.
Preface to *The Book of Runes*

God cures and the doctor sends the bill.

—Mark Twain

ver the years, I have given much thought to the possibility that the Runes could be used both to assist us in maintaining good health and to facilitate healing. In the beginning, the idea struck me as whimsical at best and, at worst, certain to raise eyebrows. Still, the notion persisted. So much has been written about illness and its cures. But what if there exists a *symbolic* component to the healing process? The influence of creative visualization on healing observed by Dr. Carl Simonton, Norman Cousins, Dr. Bernie Siegel, and others is now re-

59

ceiving serious attention from the medical establishment as well as from the general public.

Many people have found that by visualizing healthy tissue and organs, they can actually encourage the body to restore itself to health. Moreover, the practice of repeating positive affirmations has been shown, through the work of teachers like Louise Hay and Shakti Gawain, to be a significant adjunct to self-healing. Creative visualization, meditation, the use of positive affirmations—these are all ways of entering into direct communication with the unconscious.

There are reports of anesthetized patients hearing conversations which took place between doctors and nurses during surgery. These conversations, taken by the unconscious as literal truth, reportedly influenced the patient's state of mind in aiding or sometimes actually hindering their capacity for healing.

The other side of the coin is the so-called *placebo effect* in which a patient is subjected to a procedure that has no known therapeutic value and which, nevertheless, achieves positive results. The success of the placebo—often just a sugar pill—seems to support the possibility that we have within us a self-healing mechanism which can be mobilized when given appropriate situational and environmental cues.

R: RUNES AND HEALING

Anecdotal evidence from the Viking period indicates that the Runes were used for healing purposes. The Vikings are known to have painted runic glyphs on staves and bedsteads, on amulets and even onto the skin both as talismans of protection and for the healing of illness and wounds.

An interesting account of the use of Runes for healing is found in Chapter 72 of *Egil's Saga*. While visiting the house of Thorfinn, Egil sees a sick woman and realizes that somebody without sufficient knowledge had inscribed the wrong Runes on a piece of whalebone and then placed it in the woman's bed:

> Then quoth Egil:
> Runes shall a man not score,
> Save he can well to read them
> That a man betideth,
> On a mirk stave to stumble.
> Saw I on a scrapéd whalebone
> Ten dark staves scoréd:
> That hath to the leek-linden
> Over-long sickness broughten. *

Egil scored the appropriate runes on a stave and laid them under the sick woman's pillow. When she awakened, she said that she was healed. Used by shamans in healing rituals, the Runes were, it seems, part of the *materia medica* of the Viking era.

When I decided to write this chapter, I consulted the RuneCards with the question, "How can the Runes facilitate healing?" The Runes replied with ᛦ , *Journey Reversed*, which deals with "ruptures" and "disruptions," and calls our attention to that aspect of perfection which includes

Egil's Saga, translated by E. R. Eddison (Cambridge: Cambridge University Press, 1930), p. 83.

even our pain. The healing begins by providing new insight into how things work, and reminds us that

> what you regard as detours, inconveniences, disruptions, blockages, and even failures and deaths, will actually be *rerouting opportunities,* with union and reunion as the only abiding destinations.

The theme of communication is central to *Journey* and central to communication is the idea of *attunement,* the restoration of harmony. Good health has been described as a harmonious balance between body, mind and spirit as the condition for union with Divine Order, *when what is above and what is below are united and of one mind.* According to *Journey,* this balance is achieved by practicing right action, by removing resistances, by regulating excesses and, above all, by inviting the purpose of the Divine to manifest in our lives.

What actually made me decide to deal with the subject of Runes and healing was the number of people who have written to us about healing experiences in which the Runes have played a part. However, it is one thing to draw a RuneCard to clarify your intention on practical matters, quite another to incorporate the Runes into a healing ritual. Here is a hypothesis to account for what I have observed about Runes and healing.

> *When Runes are marked over a wound or an area of pain (on the skin, a cast, a bandage), an energy field is created within which healing is enhanced and facilitated.*

The idea of using an energy field to facilitate healing first caught my attention years ago in a report I read in a medical journal. Dr. Robert Becker, working in a veteran's hospital in upstate New York, had obtained positive results with bone fracture healing by placing the fracture in a low-frequency electric field. The field apparently acted to speed up the regeneration of bone tissue to a significant degree. The article on Becker's work came to mind when I received a letter from a thirty-seven-year-old woman named Margaret, who had suffered most of her adult life from migraine headaches.

One Woman's Headaches

After attending one of my workshops during which the therapeutic possibilities of the Runes were discussed, it occurred to Margaret to consult the Runes regarding her headaches. She had tried everything traditional medicine had to offer and nothing seemed to help. What caught my attention in her letter was the way she used her work with the Runes to expose the emotional components of her malaise.

First, she drew a Rune concerning the appropriateness of seeking assistance from the Runes. She drew ᛇ, *Eihwaz,* the Rune of Defense, and noted particularly the counsel about avoiding stressful situations that created the blockage she identified with her headaches. Margaret wrote, "To me this Rune said that there were three elements to consider: (1) the headache, (2) the cause of the headache, and (3) the message of the Rune. *Defense* counseled me to look at my relationships, at situations that angered me, areas where I was not being true to myself. I made a clear decision to let go of whatever was causing the migraines."

Next, she asked for a Rune that would help her to end the headaches. She drew $\lrcorner$, *Flow Reversed.* She read the appropriate passage and thought particularly about ways in which she had been trying to exceed her own strength, to do the impossible. Before going to bed, she inked the two Runes onto her temples. In the morning, she left the faintest trace of the Runes on her face.

"During the following days," Margaret reported, "on bits of paper, I'd doodle the Rune for *Flow* over and over again, sometimes drawing it on a simple picture of my face. I even kept the Rune in my hand while I was driving. Finally, I made myself a *Laguz* pendant and hung it around my neck. I also did a lot of thinking about my relationship with my husband and children. And about everything I could see in my life that wasn't working. I began to make changes. Soon the headaches came less frequently. Now I rarely get a migraine, but when I feel one coming on, I make myself slow down. I take the time to consider my frustrations, my unexpressed feelings, my unmet needs—in fact, everything that could give a person a nasty headache! Then I'll pick a Rune and think about its message."

What are we to make of Margaret's use of the Runes? Perhaps, quite simply, she was at a point in her life when she was ready to face the issues that were causing her distress. One thing is certain: A migraine headache is not likely to be made worse if you consult the Oracle. You may discover, as Margaret did, that the Runes help you to focus on the underlying causes of your problem. Perhaps the Runes help to restore balance in ways we do not yet understand.

A warning is obligatory here. Please be mindful that *the Runes are not offered as a substitute for your doctor. If you require conventional medical attention, do not hesitate to seek it.*

Runes and The Irvine Method

When, over a period of time, a subject like Runes and healing persists in claiming my attention, I watch for opportunities to test it out in my own life. The criteria I apply are simple: 1) there must be genuine need; 2) the results must be verifiable and also, to some degree, measurable; 3) the technique must be repeatable.

The perfect opportunity for me to use the Runes to facilitate healing presented itself in 1987 while I was in Mexico on a pilgrimage. It was a blistering hot afternoon in Palenque, and I was just completing the descent from a steep pyramid. Stepping off the final stone, I gave my left ankle a vicious twist. It was the kind of twist where, for a moment, the ankle goes horizontal and takes the entire body's weight. The pain was excruciating.

By good fortune, my climbing companion was Dr. David Irvine, a general practitioner from Ashland, Oregon. As I staggered toward a stone wall to sit down, David seized my arm and commanded, "Walk!" He half-carried me my first few steps. I could hardly see through the curtain of pain, but I was conscious of his voice saying, "Visualize your ankle completely sound, the skin firm and tight, the tendons and fascia intact, smooth and slippery, irrigated by the extracellular fluid. The ligaments are whole, there is no bleeding, no swelling. The flesh is pink and healthy. . . ."

While David's voice kept up its litany of instructions, in my mind's eye I saw the ankle as totally functional—healthy, intact and untraumatized. I stepped down on my left foot without flinching, merely accepting the pain. I can't tell you whether it was seconds that passed or minutes, but there came a moment when I realized that the pain was almost gone! I was soon walking unaided, allowing the left ankle to take my entire weight. When I looked, I could detect only a slight puffiness around the ankle.

David gave me two important pointers. First, you must begin the visualization procedure *instantly,* even as the shock of the trauma is being communicated to the brain. Second, you must be willing to ignore the onslaught of pain. When I thought about it later, it seemed to me that the visualization and affirmations had served to short-circuit the perception of injury, to replace it with a different metaphor—that of a healthy ankle.

When I had completed my walking meditation, I sat down and pulled out my bag of Runes. Focusing on the restored ankle, I drew ⟩ , *Eihwaz, Defense,* Avertive Powers, and, using a felt-tipped pen, inked it on the left side of the ankle bone. I replaced the stone in the bag, drew again, and this time got ᚾ , *Nauthiz,* the Rune of *Constraint,* Necessity, Pain, and inked the glyph on the right side of the bone. I looked up to find David watching me. "Why not?" he said, smiling, "There's still a lot we don't know about healing."

Afterward, David told me he had successfully used this visualization technique on a number of occasions. I felt excited by what had happened, the natural way in which it had occurred. People are said to talk effectively to their cabbages and zinnias. Why then should we not talk to cysts, migraines, tumors and lesions? Indeed, why not to sprained ankles?

But I needed further validation of the Irvine Method. "One-to-a-hundred is easy," my grandfather used to say. "Now, zero-to-one, *that* sometimes takes a bit of work." Well, I had the zero-to-one part. About a year after the first ankle twist, I did it again, to the same ankle, although in a less exotic setting, in London. I stepped off the curb in

Oxford Street and the ankle buckled. Again the wrench was agonizing. But even as the wave of pain was still rising to engulf my senses, I began: *My ankle is healthy, the tendons perfect, the blood flow to the ligaments is normal, there is no swelling. . . .*

I made my way slowly along the sidewalk with the crowd heading for the tube station. I refused to limp or favor the ankle. What happened was wonderful. In less than a block of steady walking and issuing instructions to my unconscious, the pain started to fade. As my walking got easier, I began to breathe regularly, deeply. I felt a thrill of victory.

Because I didn't have the Runes with me, I imagined a blank stone and waited for a glyph to appear in my mind. Up came ⟨ , *Opening.* Mentally, I saw the glyph inked onto the outside of my ankle, and imagined the ankle bathed in golden light, swathed in a healing fire inside and out. I erased the mental image and asked for another Rune. This time it took longer. I was buying my subway ticket when ⌐ , *Flow,* appeared on my imaginary stone. As I visualized a drawing of the symbol on the inside of my ankle, I saw the blood pumping through the ankle, bathing and soothing it. Riding down the escalator, I gave thanks. Not just because I was free of pain, but also for the opportunity to test what I had learned.

Several months ago, I again twisted that vulnerable left ankle. Without a moment's hesitation, I activated the Irvine Method with the same positive results. The ordinariness of that third twist—I was merely walking along a mountain trail—made me wonder why it had happened. I wasn't being careless. I wasn't tired. When I had completed the routine of telling my ankle how healthy it was, I took my RuneCards out of my backpack, drew two cards and inked the glyphs onto my skin. I'd begun to think of the process as a kind of oracular Ace bandage.

The cards I drew made me laugh. They were *Possessions* and *Protection*. My knapsack was loaded with things that I didn't really need on the hike, including two books; two water containers, both still full; a length of rope and a flashlight (it was early afternoon); a camera still set for the first picture. *Possessions*. And as for *Protection,* the commentary provides a fitting text to underscore the Irvine Method: "If you find yourself feeling pain, observe the pain, stay with it."

Again and again, I find myself surprised by the playfulness of the Runes, and by their invariable ability to hit the mark. What a marvelous ally the unconscious can be.

This is the first time I've written about the Irvine Method. I have a hunch that it could help with bee stings, knocks on the head and countless other traumas to which the flesh is heir. At the very least, I see it as a way to replace the old template of passivity in the face of pain and illness with a new one of active participation in the process of our own healing.

Once again, however, let me repeat that this technique is *not intended as a substitute for consulting a physician when reason and circumstances indicate.*

In Conclusion

Available information on the practice of runic healing is, for the most part, anecdotal. Perhaps it is well that it remains so, for this is not the province of medical science, but rather a folk art at the disposal of all whose Faith is not confined by the strictures of conventional medicine.

We hear more and more talk these days about "healing energy," about the laying on of hands by body workers, clergy, and by members of the medical profession—a doctor's touch, a nurse's touch. It is good to remember that we are made in God's image and that we have available to us, at all times, the power of the mind which, when coupled to the will, and the heart, can move mountains.

If I can do nothing else, whenever my path intersects the path of another who is hurting, I send Light. I send Light when an ambulance passes me on the street or when I hear of a friend who is in the hospital far away. I send Light when the evening news shows me starvation in Africa, brutality in the Middle East, warfare and suffering wherever it may be. Sending cash donations may be beyond your means but you can never overdraw a Light account.

The why and how of Rune healing matter less than the fact that something positive is accomplished. Select the Runes, use them, record the process and learn from it. Consider the appropriateness of any Rune reading. Does it serve you? Does it open your mind to a course of action that might otherwise have eluded you? Is the healing time accelerated enough beyond the normal curve to surprise your doctor? The ℞ is yours to concoct and administer. Perhaps you will let us at the RuneWorks know your results.

As always, common sense and reason form the cornerstones of any useful practice. And with them, there are the articles of our Faith. The prescription to which I hold most strongly advocates that we always place everything for which we yearn—our desires, our petitions, our hopes for a saner, healthier, richer life—in the Light. I know of no stronger petition to support that prescription than the prayer voiced in the text for the twentieth Rune: *I will to will Thy Will.*

THE WAY OF THE WARRIOR

If you keep your spirit correct
from morning till night,
accustomed to the idea of death
and resolved on death,
thus becoming one
with the way of the warrior,
you can pass through life
with no possibility of failure
and perform your office properly.

—Yamamoto Tsunenori, seventeenth century,
Hidden Leaves

Eighth-century Rune Stone
Thornhill, Yorkshire, England

5
RUNES AND DREAMING

What you are is God's gift to you. What you make of yourself is your gift to God.

—Nurse Joan Harker

In dreams begin responsibilities.

—William Butler Yeats

once met an old man in the Australian outback who told me how, since childhood, he had "invited dreaming" to come to him. The practice of inviting a dream to provide answers and to assist us in resolving problems in our daily lives has been with us from the beginning. We conceive the future in our dreams and discover in them clues for understanding the past. A powerful creative tool, the dream is the voice of the unconscious, the most ancient of Oracles.

Runes to Dream By

The procedure used for this exercise is very simple. Just before going to sleep, pick a RuneCard. Meditate on its image. Consider how the interpretation applies to what is happening in your life at present. Place the card under your pillow. Or copy the glyph onto a piece of paper, ball it up and hold the paper in your hand as you fall asleep.

You may have an issue in mind or you may simply ask for a dream that will speak to what you need to know for your life now. If a dream comes to you, the first thing to do when you awake is record as much of the dream as you can remember. After receiving a dream, you may elect to choose two RuneCards to complete a Three-Rune Spread.

Through this technique, you can influence your dreaming by focusing your unconscious on some aspect of your life that requires attention or healing. The resulting dreams and insights are often profound. Which brings me to a night not long ago, when I felt a strong urge to pick a Rune and ask for a dream.

Inviting the Dream

I asked to be given a dream that would serve me in relation to the mounting pressure I was feeling to complete this manuscript. A dream to guide me in deepening my work with the Oracle, and strengthen in me the will to serve the Divine. A dream for the next stage of the journey.

The RuneCard I drew was ᚱ , *Raido Reversed,* the Rune of *Journey,* Communication, Union and Reunion. Even when upright, *Journey* offers a serious admonition to "neutralize your refusal to let right action flow through you." Reversed, *Journey* reminds me that this is a time when "ruptures are more likely than reconciliations" and that the requirements of my process may totally disrupt what I had intended. For a while, I sat with the card in my hand, thinking about its powerful implications. Then I copied the upside-down "R" onto a bit of paper, clasped it in my left hand and turned off the light.

The Snake in the Basement

At 3:55 A.M., I awoke with a start from a dream so vivid that I was actually breathless. Here is the dream as I wrote it down moments after I awoke:

In the dream, people are shouting and dashing about in panic. The room I am in is underground, with concrete walls, floor and ceiling, well lit, scattered with tables, boxes, wrapped objects, obviously a storage room. "The snake! The snake!" someone is shouting. There is a snake loose on the floor, slithering beneath the tables. I hear its sound: a vibrant twanging, like a rattlesnake's sound amplified electronically. I peer under a long table and see the snake coming toward me, its eyes red, its body an undulating rainbow of colors—blue, yellow, orange, green—glowing with malevolent energy.

As the snake reaches me, I swiftly move forward and plant my left foot on its head. I am wearing thick furry bedroom slippers almost as large as snowshoes. The snake thrashes under my foot, its body pulsating as I keep pressure on the angry head. I shout for assistance but suddenly the cement room is empty. I am alone.

There is nothing to do but continue to ride the snake. Its strength is such that it actually moves me from my original position. The snake's body begins to swell, engorged, ballooning. My hand finds a big stick and I bash the snake, break its skin. The guts ooze and spurt and the snake starts to die. Still I stand on it, riding it, until at last the viper is dead, emptied, flat.

Using the stick, I roll the skin out. I must preserve it. A small dog appears, a friendly mutt, wanting some of the snake. I give the dog a whack with the stick. It looks at me, eyes hurt, as if to say it was only being a dog. Then from behind me a feral cat rushes in and, dragging away a heavy piece of the snake, starts to escape. I seize the cat, wresting the snake's body from its jaws; the cat bites me. A smaller cat makes off with another piece of snake through a hole in the concrete wall. I reach in after it, grasp its bony flanks and am bitten again. I hold on and the cat's teeth cling to my hand, but I recover the section of the snake. I shout and the cat lets go of my hand and disappears through the wall.

All that day, I thought about the dream's significance. The storeroom is clearly a metaphor for my personal unconscious, and it's fairly cluttered, although not crammed full, merely chaotic. There is clear and present danger manifest in the snake. Since ancient times, the snake has represented healing, empowerment, the feminine, the creative life force, which if not honored can also be dangerous. There is a mystery here and a paradox: The empowerment—the snake—has to be contained, even destroyed.

In the dream, I am doing battle—fighting to save *my* skin! A part of me, the feminine, so long contained and suppressed, now has to be taken on in open combat, in bloody battle. This totally irreverent, destructive aspect of the feminine is an aspect that I must recognize, reckon with and embrace as my own.

And what about the dog and the cats? What is their function in my snake dream? The dog and the cats represent the bridge between the human and the more primitive animal instincts. But their power has been domesticated and does not serve me. So I had to fight them off to preserve and honor the deeper, more primitive power carried by the snake.

While writing this book, I am under the very real pressure of a deadline *(Cross it, you're dead!)* and that pressure has created a form with a shape of its own—the angry snake. I've let myself be tyrannized by deadlines, made myself the slave of something artificial, foisted upon me by my conditioning. The bloody part of the dream—the gore, the violence—states in no uncertain terms what the anima, the Muse, thinks about deadlines. In the dream a different force is trying to come through.

"Listen," the Muse is saying, "I gave you this insight to work with the Runes, so don't put me in some little box you call 'time.' What you call 'the work' is not limited to this book. It involves all aspects of creativity, of cherishing life, of healing, of love for people. The Runes are only a vehicle."

At this time in my life, according to the dream, I must face the dangerous and mysterious aspects of creativity. I am alone in the storeroom and there is no one to help me. "You don't call me in and then turn me off!" the Muse is saying. "I'll send you snakes! I'll clean out your storeroom!"

The snake dream seemed to me to indicate a powerful intersection between dream and myth, between the demands of the psyche and the realities of daily living. The Rune that evoked the dream speaks to the need for integration between as yet unreconciled aspects of my nature.

Three-Card Spread

If I let *Journey Reversed* represent the *Overview* of my situation, what is the *Challenge* I am facing? Before I fell asleep again, I drew another card. This time I didn't look; I just put it under my pillow. Nor did I dream. In the morning, when I awoke, I discovered that the Challenge Card was ⋔,

Strength, which speaks of "termination and new beginnings" and of "opportunity disguised as loss." A radical transformation is necessary, the text is telling me, an upheaval at the deepest level of my psyche—in the basement storeroom, the precinct of the snake.

And then I had a thought. *What if the snake was not attacking me?* I visualized it again gliding toward me over the concrete floor, as if in a film with the sound off. The pulsating body of the snake is beaded with a rainbow of colors and I can see its beauty. My fear of the snake is gone. And yet I had killed it without hesitation. Clearly, in the dream, that is what I needed to do.

Three days later I reached the point of seeing still another choice. What if I had welcomed the snake, heard its rattling as the sound of a sacred rattle, seen its electric body as Divine energy ready for the dance? Could that snake have been coming to show me the Dance of Creation, the Dance of the Feminine?

Assisted by the Runes, the dream has now resolved itself into a parable of *Journey* and *Strength.* So I picked a third card, for *The Course of Action Called For,* and drew X̄ , *Partnership.*

Taken together, the message of the three Runes is clear: *The disruption of my process, letting go of old outmoded ways of doing things, provides me with the strength that will, in time, nourish my capacity for partnership. Partnership between equals—partnership with myself, with the feminine and, ultimately, with the Divine.*

As I write, I can still call up the vision of that snake, its red eyes fixed on mine, its body rattling and glowing as it glides straight toward me. I can feel the life force, the wisdom that calls for the shedding of the old. But I am in a cycle of productive work. At such a time, it is difficult to surrender to the snake.

And then I remembered *Separation,* the fourth RuneCard with its image of a snake shedding its skin. I have a feeling that the snake will be back. Next time, perhaps I will invite her to dance.

Exercises

I think of dreams like the one described above—dreams that occur at moments of transition and transformation, dreams sufficiently potent to lift the lid off the psyche—as *life intersection dreams.*

You may want to record your dreams by keeping a Dream Journal. Begin your journal by listing the conditions, habits or aspects of character that are no longer suitable to the person you are becoming. List any changes you *know* you wish to make in your life, your work, your relationships with others. Then draw a RuneCard—or a stone—and ask for a dream. Read the interpretation for that Rune and use the text for guidance in understanding your dream. If you feel the need for further clarification, draw again.

I have found that *asking* is the essential act. You may not receive a dream the first night you request it. However, you can always ask again or, having made your request, know that you will be served by the unconscious in its own time, in God's time. We are not responsible for the receiving, finding or opening. Only for the asking, seeking and knocking.

Major dreams resemble major earthquakes in that, following such dreams, there are likely to be dream echos and dream variations for nights to come. These aftershocks tend to occur over time and in descending magnitude on the

Richter Scale of dreams. The thematic content of the dreams may vary, but their relevance will be apparent to you when you are watching for it.

If you are willing to listen, your dreams will continue to speak to you from the realm of possibilities. And the Runes will serve you in sorting between pathways, in dreams as in waking life.

WINNEBAGO INDIAN PRAYER

O Great Spirit,
Whose voice I hear in the wind,
And whose breath gives life to all the world,
Hear me! I am small and weak.
I need your strength and wisdom.
Let me walk in beauty and make my eyes
Ever behold the red and purple sunset.
Make my hand respect the things you have made
And my ears sharp to hear your voice.
Make me wise so that I may understand
The things you have taught my people.
Let me learn the lessons you have hidden
In every leaf and every rock.
I seek strength, not to be greater than my brother
But to fight my greatest enemy—myself.
Make me always ready to come to you
With clean hands and straight eyes
So when life fades, like the fading sunset,
My spirit may come to you without shame.

Shaman's Mask, Jancis Salerno

6

THE CYCLE OF INITIATION

*With nothing in our hands to which we cling, with lifted
  hearts and listening minds, we pray.*

—A Course in Miracles

*Heaven bestows, but we must receive.
For what has happened, I give thanks.
For what is happening, I give praise.
For what is to happen, I have faith.*

—Akshara Noor

here are people I know who live their lives in a
constant state of initiation. The root of the word
initiation is the Latin verb *initiare,* to begin, origi-
nate, take a first step. *In the life of the spirit, we are always at the
beginning.*

The Cycle of Initiation intrigues me more and more as I
explore its applications and deeper meanings. That wasn't
always the case. As presented in the first edition of *The Book
of Runes* under the name "The Cycle of Self-Transformation," it was one Rune short. *Kano,* the Rune of Opening,

Fire, was absent. Somehow I'd forgotten to include it—my way of saying that I had not yet found the way to open the *Cycle* to creative utilization; that I needed more Light in order to come to terms with this formidable aspect of Runecraft. When I saw the light, *The Cycle of Self-Transformation* became *The Cycle of Initiation*.

The launching of *The Book of RuneCards* is an appropriate time for a deeper look at the Cycle. The thirteen Runes that make up the Cycle comprise "an energy framework within the body of the runic alphabet; an armature, so to speak, facilitating and sustaining the process of self-change."

The Cycle Runes and the Story They Tell

The Thirteen Runes are ᚠ , *Signals,* ᛉ , *Separation,* ᚲ , *Strength,* ᚴ , *Initiation,* ↑ , *Constraint,* ᛉ , *Fertility,* ᚲ , *Opening,* ᛒ , *Growth,* ᛗ , *Movement,* ᚾ , *Disruption,* ᚱ , *Journey,* ᚦ , *Gateway,* ᛈ , *Breakthrough.*

Here, then, is the Cycle, in narrative form, as it relates to the journey of the Spiritual Warrior:

The self is summoned and encouraged in its natural urge to grow by the Messenger Rune, ᚠ *, which operates between the Divine and the self, through Signals, in the form of new connections that lead us onto new pathways. During this process, there occurs a peeling away, a shedding of old skins that brings about Separation and retreat,* ᛉ *, and loosens the bonds we have inherited from being in the world. Thus prepared, the self can begin to identify its true Inheritance. Once the process of change is under way, the Strength,* ᚲ *, becomes available for renewed growth into Manhood and Womanhood.*

As a natural consequence of that growth, there arrives a moment of recognition, in the form of Initiation, ᚴ *, when the release of the old makes possible a new sense of wholeness. This process occurs on an inner* level, which is why "nothing external matters here" although, clearly, there are likely to be changes in the way the self meets the challenges of daily life.

Next, the self undergoes the pain of necessary Constraint, X, in order that it may be cleansed and healed. Out of the healing arises the Fertility of new beginnings, X, and the strength becomes available to dissolve blockages that draw their energy from old habits. At this stage in the Cycle, the self experiences an Opening, ⟨, new Light by which both to receive and know the joy of giving. For the healing of the self becomes apparent when we begin to share our good fortune with others.

As the Spiritual Warrior pursues the path of the heart, Growth, B, leads to an integration of the new into a more modest, patient, and generous nature. There is no urge to turn back. The self is centered, better prepared when, with Movement, M, change and progress occur effortlessly; for as we cultivate our true nature, all else follows. Now the self is prepared for Disruption, N, as more layers of old, encrusted habits fall away. A new synthesis is possible, one marked by richer communication on the Journey, R, toward union with others and with the Higher Self, on the path toward union with the Divine.

The way stretches upward, climbing to a Gateway, Þ, a place of non-action that calls for meditation on the progress thus far. The hallmark of this second stage of initiation is integration. For beyond the Gateway awaits the place of Breakthrough, ⋈, transformation signified by radical trust. With new ability to live in the Light, and firm in its Faith, the self is once again assisted in its unbounded urge to grow.

Locating Yourself in the Cycle

Consider the narrative as it appears above. Feel into it. See if you can get a sense of where you are in the Cycle. A simple way to do this is the following.

First, separate the thirteen Cycle cards from the deck. As you mix the cards know that, rather than posing a specific issue for the Runes to comment upon, you are asking for your position in the Cycle. Next, choose a card and read its interpretation.

How does the card you have chosen speak to you about your life now? Does the text illuminate some situation that has been puzzling you? Does it help you to address an issue you have been avoiding? Do you understand why you are at this stage of Initiation?

You can also find your position by asking: *What aspect of my Nature, if modified, renewed or illuminated, will assist me in my growth?* Then choose a card and consider the interpretation.

The Indicator Card

Still another method of locating yourself in the Cycle is to mix the cards, then cut them, placing the cut portion face up. The card on top will serve as the *Indicator Card,* locating you in your current position in the Cycle.

Now, find the two cards that *precede* and *follow* the Indicator in the "Cycle of Initiation." Simply go by the numbers on the cards. Place the lower number card to the left of the Indicator Card, and the higher to the right. Let the card on the left stand for your position in the *Past,* and the card on the right for your *Future* on the path of Initiation.

Consider the transition from Past to Present to Future. How does the Past Card help to clarify your present state of being and awareness? How does the Future Card serve to encourage you? Are you ready to move ahead? Is there unfinished business from your past to which you must first attend? How does your present phase of Initiation bear upon the work you are doing, on your relationships with others and with yourself?

Sample Reading

Recently, a friend of mine tried this spread. Her Indicator Card was number twenty-two, *Breakthrough*. These are the three relevant cards:

Past   Present   Future

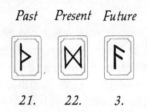

21.   22.   3.

Notice that since *Breakthrough* is the final card in the Cycle, the Future Card becomes #3, Signals. This draw was useful because it reminds us that the Cycle of Initiation does not come to an end, but represents a wheel continually turning. Here is her commentary on the three cards.

"Well, I'm definitely going through a period of major *Breakthrough,* which is requiring radical trust on my part. In *all* areas of my life—work, personal relationships, attitudes, everything's changing! My Past Rune is the *Gateway* and last year I really had to let go of my old ways of doing things. As a result, the year's end felt like a gateway leading to new beginnings. And since many of those new beginnings are in the area of communication—particularly regarding my work in publishing—drawing *Signals* as my Future Card makes perfect sense. This reading confirms what I know—that I'm right on track. My warrior nature is revealing itself, and I feel wonderful!"

This example will give you an idea of how to address the Cycle of Initiation. Obviously, it is not a technique to be used every day. The Cycle Runes are like a special navigational chart to spread out whenever the waters in which you are operating seem suddenly unfamiliar, or when local currents have swept you far off your intended course and the sky is too overcast to get your bearings. Conversely, when you are flying high and all is right with the world, there is no better time to sit in council with the Cycle Runes.

In *The Book of Runes,* it was suggested that whenever two or more of these thirteen Runes are found together in a spread "the potential for growth and integration is greatly enhanced." As you become more familiar with the thirteen, watch for their appearance in other spreads. When they cluster, regard it as a communication from the Self to the self that the work of Initiation is progressing in your life.

This brings me to an exercise, a ceremony really, that revolves around *Signals,* the Messenger Rune.

THE WHEEL OF INITIATION

Not long ago, while discussing the Runes with anthropologist Joan Halifax, I told her about the Cycle Runes and suggested the possibility of relating these thirteen Runes to the Native American Indian mandala of the Medicine Wheel. Joan's experience as a teacher of the Medicine Wheel is rich and profound. In the course of the following three days, the ceremony I call *The Wheel of Initiation* came into being.

This ceremonial spread is best undertaken by two people, one to ask the questions, the other to lay out the cards and respond. In addition to the thirteen Cycle Runes, four more cards will be drawn later from the twelve remaining in the deck. Taken together, these cards—minus the Call—represent sixteen meditations.

To begin, draw a circle, in sand or soft earth if possible, indicating the four directions, with North at the top. If more convenient, draw the circle on paper, indicating the cardinal compass points.

Next, isolate the thirteen cards that comprise the *Cycle of Initiation* from your deck. Remove ⌷ , *Signals,* the Messenger Rune, from the thirteen and place it face up in the center of the circle. This card represents the *Call,* the gate of entry, the invitation to Initiation. Turn the remaining twelve cards face down and move them around until you are no longer aware of the identity of any particular card, a reminder that the path of Initiation is always secret.

Start by selecting and placing three of the Cycle cards in a row face down in the South. This direction represents your *Child.* Similarly, select and place three cards in the North. This direction represents your *Adult.* The three cards you place in the West stand for *Initiation* or what needs to die within you. The final three cards that will lie in the East stand for your *Vision,* your life's direction.

Each group of three cards, reading from left to right, is interpreted as follows:

Left: *The card on the left represents the gift or special qualities with which you were born.*

Center: *The center card indicates how you manifest this gift in the world.*

Right: *The card on the right reveals how you express your Gift.*

This is the dynamic for each of the Four Directions. At this point, the Messenger card, standing for the Call, lies with its image revealed, while the remaining twelve cards remain face down. As you proceed through each of the four directions, physically move around the Wheel, at the same time shifting the direction of the Call card—the Rune of *Signals* in the center—so that you are always facing the Call, the gateway to Initiation.

The circle now looks like this:

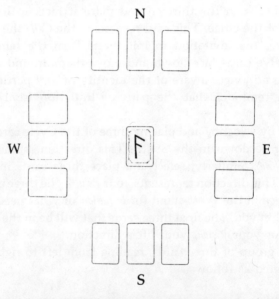

Begin in the South, with your friend asking you the first question. When the question has been asked, turn the first card (on the left) face up and, referring to the appropriate text—or if you are sufficiently familiar with the Rune interpretations, commenting from your own knowledge—respond to the question with the essence of the RuneCard just turned.

What follows is a complete outworking of The Wheel of Initiation for my life in April 1988. The questions were put to me by Joan Halifax.

In the South

1) Question: *What is the gift your child was born with?*
   Answer: 20. *Journey,* ᚱ .
   Meaning: The gift is the impulse toward union and uniting. I was in a sense born homeless, separated from my own Nature. The longing for restoration helps me to implement the gift; that and the deep knowledge that there exists, in myself, a home to which I can, indeed, return.

2) Question: *How does this gift teach your child?*
   Answer: 19. *Disruption,* ᚾ .
   Meaning: The gift teaches that facing disruption is necessary in order to achieve growth. It teaches of the need to break free from identification with material reality. It teaches me through the perspective of alienation, reversals of fortune and painful awakening.

3) Question: *How are the wounds of your child to be healed through this gift?*
   Answer: 14. *Opening,* ᚲ .

89

Meaning: By bringing Light into places where there is darkness. By examining the elements of my conditioning, which have been fragmented by disruption, I am able to discard what no longer serves me and incorporate that which I want to invest with new values.

In the North

4) Question: *What is the gift given by others that helps you to realize your full power?*
Answer: 8. *Fertility,* ᛝ .
Meaning: Through my relationships with other people, I am impelled to begin again, making new connections where the old were damaged. Others taught me how to complete things. Others recognized my gifts and insisted that I honor them.

5) Question: *What are you to learn from this gift?*
Answer: 16. *Growth,* ᛒ .
Meaning: I am to learn that Growth, achieved with modesty, leads to blossoming. I must learn gentleness and let gentleness serve to move me past my resistance. I am to develop modesty on the path of gentleness.

6) Question: *How are you to express this gift in your life?*
Answer: 22. *Breakthrough,* ᛞ .
Meaning: By transforming my life completely, making a 180-degree turn, so that the

healing of my life serves as a healing for others, possibly through my work with the Runes. That is to say, through the development of a transformational tool which, even as it serves me, serves others.

In the West

7) Question: *How do you enter into the realm of the Unknowable? the Mystery?*

Answer: 7. *Constraint,* ᛝ .

Meaning: I enter the Mystery by opening to my pain and limitation and seeing them as my teachers and guides. By recognizing my shadow—that which is disowned in my nature—I can begin to work with it and, in time, move beyond it into the Mystery.

8) Question: *How do you receive the gift of the Unknowable? That which cannot be named or described in its essence?*

Answer: 4. *Separation Reversed,* ᚷ .

Meaning: By making a total departure from old ways, old habits, old addictions and attitudes. I can, it seems, enter into the Unknowable only by leaving all else behind.

9) Question: *What is the gift that the Unknowable awakens in you?*

Answer: 17. *Movement Reversed,* ᚹ .

Meaning: The ability to help others to respond as Spiritual Warriors when their lives are in crisis. By teaching what I am learning. To regard blockage and obstacles as signs, indications to pause, go within and reconsider before taking action. Not to seek solutions but to let the solutions find me.

In the East

10) Question: *What is the gift from the past that is the source of your Vision?*

Answer: 21. *Gateway,* ᛉ .

Meaning: My vision is born from stillness. Coming to stillness is the gift from the past; learning to wait until the water is so unruffled that I can see on its calm surface the reflections of what is hidden in myself. In contemplation of the Will of the Divine for me in my life, I will see my Vision, my direction.

11) Question: *How does your Vision heal you?*

Answer: 5. *Strength,* ᚾ .

Meaning: Through discrimination and the power of discernment. By helping me to recognize that what may first appear to me as loss is actually freedom. My Vision heals me through the realization that the source of my strength lies in my ability to meet adversity.

12) Question: *How does your Vision heal others and the world?*
   Answer: 6. *Initiation,* 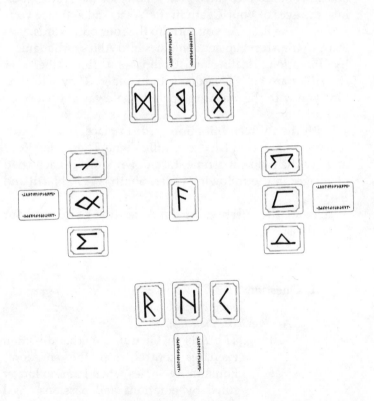 .
   Meaning: By teaching me that the old way has come to an end and that I am to live my life as Initiation. Then I will be free to share what I have learned with others.

The Questions of the Four Allies

As I mentioned earlier, there are sixteen questions. Four questions remain to be asked. They are *The Questions of the Four Allies* or Guardians. Each of the Allies controls the power of one of the Four Directions.

Working with the four Allies, you face your Fear in the South, come to recognize your Clarity in the North, look into the eyes of your Death in the West, and embrace your Power in the East. As you turn up the four outer cards, you learn to transform ancient enemies into Allies of Equanimity, Intention, Healing and Compassion. Remember that the Allies are both Guardians and Guides. They will provide you with the means to open the gateway at each stage of Initiation.

With the thirteen Initiation cards in place, twelve cards remain in the deck. Mix or shuffle them. Then select four and lay them one at a time, face down, outside each triad of images in the following order: South, West, North and East.

Here are the questions of the Allies that guard the Four Directions:

In the South

1. Question: *How can you foster in yourself steadfastness and unity of mind and heart?*

   Answer: 10. *Protection,* Ƴ .

   Meaning: The Ally or Guardian of this direction exercises control over the emotions. Equanimity comes when I am no longer ruled by emotions and passions. As I work with this Ally, I begin to acquire a sense of tranquility in my life. Anxiety and fear depart, and I no longer behave like a creature of habit and reaction.

In the North

2. Question: *What is your motivation, your true intent?*
   Answer: II. *Possessions,* 𝕀 .
   Meaning: The Guardian of the North has control of Nourishment. My intention is to seek proper nourishment so that I can, in turn, truly nourish others. This calls for dedication to my own awakening through moderation in all things.

In the West

3. Question: *What must you give away in order to heal yourself?*
   Answer: 9. *Defense,* ↓ .
   Meaning: The Guardian in the West exercises control over the meeting of obstacles. I must give away my defenses and be willing to make myself vulnerable. I am to heal myself by surrendering up my frantic traits, my lusting after outcomes, my neediness.

In the East

4. Question: *How can you live a life of compassion?*
   Answer: 13. *Harvest,* ↺ .
   Meaning: The Guardian in the East is the protector of harvests. I am to nurture and honor each being that enters my life. I am to walk the path of compassion by the

careful cultivation of patience and caring—recognizing the natural cycles of all things, practicing patience toward others and toward myself. The harvest is the compassionate life.

Here is the completed circle, with the sixteen cards placed around the central focus of the Call:

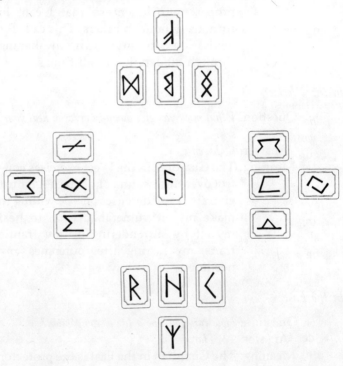

Remember, when you perform this ceremony, that you always face the Call, and you always read the RuneCards from left to right. You begin The Wheel of Initiation with all the elements hidden, except for the Call. The Call is the "given," in that by undertaking this ceremony you have recognized that you are seeking Initiation. Facing your past (in the South), recognizing it, understanding it, is the gift that allows for the cultivation and fostering of Wisdom (in the North), and in turn, for entering the Mystery (in the West) and, finally, for awakening the Vision (in the East).

Recognizing the Call

The Wheel of Initiation differs from *The Destiny Profile* (see *The Book of Runes,* pp. 70–80) in that you can undertake it more than once. And yet, there is a counsel that accompanies this set of instructions: *Do not move forward along the path of Initiation until you know that your foot is already on the path, and that you have recognized the Call.* Signs of the Call are not difficult to recognize. A life-changing illness. An emotional crisis in which you come to see your old life as meaningless. A moment when the urge to leave behind all you have believed in is so powerful that you can no longer resist seeking within for answers to questions you are truly ready to ask for the first time or in a new way.

The questions that accompany the Wheel of Initiation are preparation for seeking what is called, in the Native American Indian world, *medicine:* an empowering energy for the work you have to do on yourself, in your life. In its way, The Wheel of Initiation is akin to the Vision Quest. The ceremony can serve to orient you according to your current state of awareness. The Call asks that you undertake first this . . . then this . . . then this . . . then this, in ever-widening circles of movement, commitment, and realization.

*　*　*

Much more could be said about each of the cards and their placement on The Wheel of Initiation. When Joan Halifax showed me the way to reconcile the Viking Runes with the Medicine Wheel, I understood something fundamental about my Faith and the source from which it draws strength and nourishment. I am acquiring a new respect for the blockages on my path. I am beginning to welcome, as challenges, those things which once dismayed me. And I am coming to embrace the wisdom implicit in the first words of the ninth Rune: *As we are tested we fund the power to avert blockage and defeat.*

In undertaking this ceremony, you are recognizing that the path of Initiation never ceases. You may be drawn to use this spread time and again. When you live your life as Initiation, every moment is a messenger calling you to awaken to the hidden power of the ordinary. The Wheel of Initiation is a rite of passage dedicated to the awakening of the Spiritual Warrior within each of us.

PREDICTION

Someday,
after we have mastered the winds,
the waves, the tides and gravity,
we shall harness for God
the energies of love.
Then, for the second time
in the history of the world,
we will have discovered fire.

—Teilhard de Chardin

The Gokstad long ship. Ninth century.
Viking Ship Museum, Oslo, Norway.

7

RUNES, FAITH AND PREDICTION

Quench not the Spirit. Despise not prophecyings. Prove all things; hold fast that which is good.

—I Thessalonians 5:19–21

Through your awareness of God's power at work in and through¹ you, you know that new avenues of good are opening for you. You do your part by affirming the truth of and giving thanks for right opportunities.

—The Daily Word

ne of the articles of my Faith concerns the legitimacy of thought for the future. When deciding what to include in *The Book of Runes,* I steadfastly refused to consider using the Runes for prediction. It didn't feel right to me to do so. I have always believed that the future is not our concern and that God's Will for our lives is made known in the present moment. And besides, when did you last make a mistake in the future?

The Fifth Race at Warrnambool

In all my years of working with the Runes, I have never knowingly consulted the Oracles to predict a future event or outcome—with one minor exception. I was being interviewed on a radio show in Melbourne, Australia. The host pushed a folded newspaper in front of me and I found myself staring at that afternoon's racing form for a local track called Warrnambool. He wanted me to use the Runes to pick the winner for the fifth race. I said that wasn't my line of work. He said, "Aw, go on, just this once." I can't tell you why I complied, unless it was for the way things turned out. So I drew a Rune from my bag and got *Fehu*, ᚠ, the Rune of *Possessions* and Nourishment.

We went over the list of horses in the fifth race. They were: Mr. Spence, Wild Native, Sing for Supper, Battle So Big, Matchem Rocky (scratched), French Veneer, Lady Sheila and Jetter.

When we finished looking at the entries, I confessed that I saw no clues. At the host's suggestion, we scanned the list of jockeys' names: Green, Delaney, Murphy, Ace, Cannon, Julius, Griffiths and O'Sullivan. Still nothing.

I read over the pertinent passages in the interpretation for the eleventh Rune: "ambition satisfied, love fulfilled, rewards received . . . nourishment, from the most worldly to the sacred and Divine . . . wealth and possessions . . ." I still couldn't find a fit and, with a sense of relief, I bowed out. To consult the Runes for picking a horse seemed to me an improper use of the Oracle.

The following day, back in Sydney, I received a call from the radio talk show host.

"It was right in front of us all the time," he said, laughing, "but you wouldn't see it."

"Wouldn't see what?"

"I missed it too. The winner was Sing for Supper—get it? Supper? *Nourishment?* And the odds were forty-to-one. Well, what do you say to that?"

I said I wish I'd had a fiver on the horse.

The Pack-or-Path Test

Again and again the issues of forecasting and prediction have come up with regard to the Runes. Over the years a number of people have written to the RuneWorks describing their use of the Oracle to prepare themselves to meet the future. Now the time seems at hand to face directly what I have avoided. My reason for writing this chapter is to meet that challenge.

A psychiatrist friend once told me, "Before I see a patient, I always pick a Rune to get a fix on where he or she is in their process." Some people draw a Rune upon meeting a person who might be a potential partner. Others will consult the Runes for the best possible outcome before embarking on a journey or a new project. Here we are already in the borderland of prediction.

I believe I have finally found a track that permits me to confront the issue of Runes and the future and not be untrue to my Faith. I call it the *Pack-or-Path Test.* The criterion for using the Runes as they relate to a future situation is the following:

> *Is what I am asking intended to achieve material gain? To provide me with something that I can carry in my Pack? Or will what I am asking increase my Faith and move me forward along my Path in service to the Will of the Divine?*

If the former, turning to the Runes would be inappropriate. If the latter, then you are calling upon the Oracle for aid in serving the highest good. Consult the RuneCards regarding issues whose outcome will support the growth of the human spirit. This would constitute legitimate and creative use of prediction with any Oracle.

In order to discern the difference between creature comforts and the needs of the soul, ask yourself, *Is this for my Pack, or is it for my Path?*

Prediction and the Mechanics of Time

My friend Randall de Mattei has been studying extraordinary human abilities for many years. Recently, I asked him for a briefing on how people see into the future. What follows is a synopsis of our conversation.

There are two fundamental ways to conceptualize seeing into the future. The traditional approach maintains that everything is preordained, already in place, and that some-how the gifted person gets access to that record. A more contemporary view holds that no part of the future is fixed in any way, rather it is created by random collisions of events and objects, and that present events shape the future by affecting that randomness.

When gifted people look into the future, they begin with their understanding of what's happening *now,* in part play-ing that out to a *likely* outcome, in part getting a glimpse of a *possible* outcome, then putting both together in an intuitive inference. They can be right, wrong, or partially right. They may give too much weight to something they see in current time, believe it will play out a certain way, and be off in their timing.

Viewers of the future have to be able to get out of their own way, otherwise their understanding can be distorted by their desires. Intent, shared commitment, and desire can act as powerful screens so that, when you look into the future, you get pulled off onto a preferred thought form that will send you down a biased track.

The question remains: *How do you create your own reality?* Accepting responsibility for being able to affect your future by seeing a desired outcome is the first step. The next step is to undertake the work to bring that future into being. Then take the next step, and the next, doing what is called for until the desired outcome is realized. If you sit still and do nothing, the future *will* come, but it may look radically different from what you had hoped for or intended.

There is no formula for predicting the future. What I am attempting to describe is an intuitive art, not a science. And there is often an element of play involved—sacred play—a mixture of reverence and irreverence. So watch for puns, both visual and linguistic, that may provide you with useful clues. A case in point: the fifth race at Warrnambool, the Rune of Nourishment and *Possessions,* and a horse named Sing for Supper.

RUNES AND INTENTION

When you stop to think about it, *setting your intention is actually a form of prediction.* For the setting of intention in the present will help to determine your future position in any situation, in the same way that varying your heading by two degrees as you leave port will make a significant difference in your position five hundred miles out to sea. Creating the future begins with action taken in the present. Using the RuneCards to train your intuitive knowing— really your ability to *listen*—and then bringing that knowledge to bear on your life *now* is a fundamental way of influencing the future.

Exercise

Visualize clearly a goal that you wish to achieve. Go over it in your mind in detail, considering its *distinctive features.* In other words, create a scenario in which events, actors and outcomes are all in place, and the goal you wish to achieve is already actualized, real and operating in your life.

Next, use the RuneCards to clarify your intention. Ask the following three questions, drawing a card for a commentary on each question in turn. After you draw a card for one question, replace it in the deck so that you are always using a complete deck.

1. *Of what do I need to be mindful to ensure that the result of my intention will be a source of genuine satisfaction in my life?*
2. *How can my intention be better conceived so that it will benefit all those concerned?*
3. *How does my intention serve the highest good?*

I suggest that the setting of intentions is the essence of the prediction process. Without clearly defined intentions and goals, you remain at the mercy of your old habit patterns. Intention setting is an exercise in behavior modification and a stimulus for self-change.

In undertaking this exercise you are actually assuming responsibility for the way you go through the world. By using the RuneCards in an advisory capacity, you are not attempting to "know the future" but rather to invoke the joy of right opportunities in your life.

With clarity and through prayer, set your feet on the path toward the realization of your desired future. The function of the RuneCards is both to encourage you to look within, and to encourage you to take responsibility for creating your reality. At the same time, remember to be open to the play of the Divine in your life and welcome any surprises that come to you.

THE ARCHER ON THE TOWER

In every life there come moments when we are played out, when the energy to continue along a familiar path is exhausted; times when we are feeling so overwhelmed by dissatisfaction that we can't even imagine a better future. Working with the Runes at such low moments has taught me a valuable lesson. It has become my practice, when things look bleakest, to release my hold on the situation, empty my mind and ask: *What do I need to focus my attention on now?*

How do you get your bearings when your compass is broken? The RuneCards can be particularly helpful when you need direction and encouragement. Give yourself space. Try something you have never tried before. On occasion, I have used the Native American Indian Medicine Wheel and the Four Directions to orient myself. I would like to tell you about a friend, a computer scientist, who came up with his own interpretation of the Four Directions, and about the technique he created for working with the RuneCards.

At forty, Jack was truly at a crossroads. He had given years of his life to a company that had recently fallen apart and was now bankrupt. He was left out in the cold with no job. Because of the unusual nature of his work, few opportunities for meaningful employment in his field existed. His life seemed to have lost its direction.

He was feeling depressed and obsessing about his future when an image came to mind of a stone tower. An archer was standing on the top of the tower. He had a bow and a quiver of arrows and was firing the arrows in the Four Directions.

The image, Jack told me, seemed particularly appropriate at the time. Was he to leave the work of years behind and seek employment in a different field? Was he to strike out on his own, start a new company and begin at the beginning? Or was he to give it all up, do nothing, take his life's savings and hit the road?

Several weeks later, Jack called again to tell me that he had pursued the image, "gathered up the four arrows," and found that each one had a symbol on it. The one fired to the North by the archer carried a lightning bolt. The arrow of the South showed a red circle on a field of black. The one fired to the East bore an image of the sun. And on the arrow fired to the West, the stone tower.

He interpreted the four symbols in the following way:

In the North: *(Lightning Bolt) Self-Responsibility*
In the South: *(The Circle) The Mystery, the Unconscious, the Intuitive*
In the East: *(The Sun) Life Energy, Creative Ideas*
In the West: *(The Tower) Home, Hearth, Security*

Taking a moment to compose himself and let go of all conflicting thoughts and emotions, he focused on the issue: *What action, if taken now, will create the best outcome in the future?*

Selecting one RuneCard for each of the Four Directions, Jack laid them out, face down, North, South, East, West. When he turned the cards over, this was the layout:

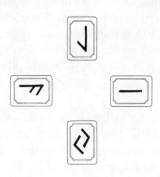

He interpreted the meaning of the four RuneCards in the following way:

North: *"Flow* is in the North, which tells me that the easiest way to go, the path of least resistance, is to work for somebody else."

South: *"Harvest* is in the place of the Intuitive, which to me means wait for the unconscious to tell me what to do."

East: "The place of *Standstill* is not where I want to go—that's where I am now! At the same time, I'm attracted by the path of least resistance in the North."

West: "The Rune of *Signals,* in the West, is calling me to take action that will establish my security.

Perhaps in the West I won't get an immediate harvest, but I feel its pull. Maybe I'll start my own business out there. And I like what I see in the image of the RuneCard—the rising star, my star rising, with the bird bringing the branch to tell me that the bad times are over. So maybe I'll go West by Northwest, follow the bird with the branch and watch for *Signals.* I've been thinking a lot about Seattle lately."

In the end, Jack took his savings and went to visit some old friends in Seattle. On his second day in town, he was introduced to the owner of a company "whose computer consultant had just been shot in the back with an arrow by his twelve-year-old son, who was wearing—on my honor, it's God's truth!—a green Robin Hood costume that had been given to him for his birthday."

Jack stood in for the injured computer programmer and began doing part-time consulting for other small entrepreneurial businesses in the area. Three months later, he started his own company.

Thinking over the bizarre twist of fate that set Jack on his new path, I remembered years ago reading in a book on megalithic cultures that the people who preceded the Etruscans were known only by the stone towers they left behind. And by a single piece of bronze work, found in Sardinia, showing an archer.

The boy archer in the Robin Hood suit. The Archer on the Tower.

Faith and Prediction

The objective, when working with the RuneCards and prediction, is not to influence or get "an edge" on future events, but rather to receive guidance for right action in the present, using the future as evidence to support your intention.

For the most part, we are asked to live by Faith, trusting in God without having to know the future. A key question to ask yourself before turning to the RuneCards on a matter of future concern is: *Will the knowledge I seek to learn about the future serve to strengthen my Faith?*

The use of the RuneCards for prediction is, for me, a recent undertaking and very much in the experimental stage. To date I have used the Runes as an adjunct to prediction only sparingly in my own life. As appropriate occasions arise, you may wish to record your predictive insights, then watch to discover how they correlate with actual future events in your life. We at the RuneWorks would appreciate hearing about your experiences.

Only remember, when you are tempted to bring the future into your circle of present counsel, to ask yourself: *Is what I want for my Pack or for my Path?*

You'll know the answer in your heart.

CREATION

What do you suppose creation is?
What do you suppose will satisfy the soul,
except to walk free and own no superior?
What do you suppose I would intimate to you
in a hundred ways,
but that man or woman is as good as good?
And that there's no God any more divine than Yourself?
And that that is what the oldest and newest myths finally mean?
And that you or anyone must approach creation
through such laws?

—Walt Whitman

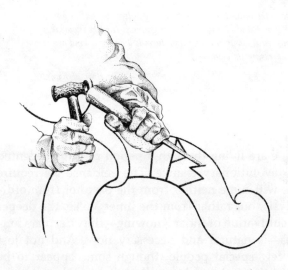

8

CREATING THE
ORACULAR INDIVIDUAL

*Living in this chaotic environment, I've come to realize that unless you
have a very close relationship with God and unless you personally are
living as exemplary a life as you can, then what you say to people isn't
going to have much of an impact.*

—John Cardinal O'Connor

*As we start to make contact with our Knowing Selves, we will begin to
hear messages of profound beauty and true usefulness. For like snowflakes
and fingerprints, each of our oracular signatures is a one-of-a-kind aspect
of Creation addressing its own.*

—The Book of Runes

e are living through a period of unprecedented
evolutionary change. The guidance we require
will come neither from the past nor from ordinary analysis, but rather from the Inner Voice, the deeper
mind. So cultivation of Inner Knowing—the Oracular Consciousness—is natural and necessary now. And not just
among a few special people, though some appear to be
more gifted than others. After all, there are Olympic ath-
letes, why not Olympic Oracles? But the truth is, *everyone*

is capable of oracular insight. At first, the experience may be fleeting, but by keeping a journal you can follow the train of your Inner Voice and, in time, became a master of *Inner Listening.* All you have have to do is quiet yourself and listen. *Be still and know that I am God.*

Out of that stillness, in our time, are emerging two distinct voices that can be regarded as oracular. One is the *channeled voice,* which has lately been getting considerable press, both good and bad. Less prominent, less celebrated, perhaps because its emergence is more organic, is the voice of the *Oracular Individual.* For the former, there exists a flourishing market in workshops, how-to books, audio- and videotapes. There is as yet no handbook on how to become an Oracular Individual.

Perhaps this is a blessing. The path of the Oracular Individual requires a commitment to self-discovery and personal experiment. It is a practice no less than sitting meditation is a practice. Its ground is as venerable as the sacred texts on which Western spiritual tradition is founded. When Old Testament prophets spoke, they were not working from prepared scripts. The voice in which they spoke was the Oracular Voice.

There is always a powerful instinct among defenders of the sacred to tolerate no new contributions. "Add not a word to what is written here!" seems to be the edict, and it is usually signed for God by the priesthood of record. Well, something is afoot. There is a new breeze tugging at the ancient banners of the oracular, a feeling that deeper wisdom is available to each of us, if only we can access its blessings.

Of the many people I have encountered who have successfully incorporated oracular practice into their lives, by far the most creative and articulate is author and futurist

Barbara Marx Hubbard.* Her dedication to the birth of a new Planetary Society recommends her as a role model. What follows is the result of a series of conversations out of which came the first sketches of a *blueprint for creating the Oracular Individual.*

In 1966, in a meditation, Barbara Marx Hubbard asked the question, "What in our age is comparable to the birth of Christ? What is our story?" As she describes it: "I experienced our planet as a living organism struggling to cooperate. I saw a Light in space so powerful that it caught everyone's eye at once. That act of shared attention allowed Love to course through the body of us all. In my vision, the barriers all around the planet collapsed. There was a rush across borders. None of the old separations held. Simultaneously, we all smiled a planetary smile, and the smile opened our collective eyes. Then I heard the words: *Our story is a birth. We are the body. One integrated body. We are one. We are whole. We are universal. We are good.*"

What she heard was a voice speaking of the Divine Self, of the Christ as our potential self. It is a voice that explains the prophetic tradition of the New Testament as "coded evolution." It speaks of a time when we will all be changed; when, as the result of a general planetary rise in consciousness, the Armageddon scenario will no longer be necessary. Instead, we will experience a *Planetary Pentecost,* comparable to the first Pentecost, when all those gathered in the upper room heard the Divine Voice, heard it speak of the mighty works of God in their own language. The new Pentecost will be a mass oracular experience. This is the alternative

*Barbara Marx Hubbard, *The Hunger of Eve.* East Sound, Washington: Sweet Forever Publishing, 1989.

to Armageddon—mass healings, mass transformations, the experience of Light.

In order to foster conscious awareness of her own oracular insights, Barbara Marx Hubbard takes long walks, clears her mind of all thought, and invites the Inner Voice to speak. What she hears, she dictates into a tape recorder and then plays the recording back. This practice has accustomed her to hearing the Inner Voice. She has discovered that *the Inner Voice is always on;* she maintains that *it is always on in everybody.* The problem is that that we only listen occasionally. In our normal waking state, we are actually asleep. By going within, and expressing what we find there, we awaken the cellular memory of our connectedness to God.

The challenge, therefore, is to develop a dual consciousness: to be able to move in a rational, linear world and yet hear the Inner Voice at all times. The goal is to learn to speak to others Higher Self to Higher Self.

Barbara Marx Hubbard has developed a technique which she calls the *Higher Self Dialogue.* It has some of the elements of a Quaker meeting, of speaking from silence. No going into trance, no out-of-body rock 'n' roll, just allowing Inner Knowing to be expressed. When you experience this dialogue with two or three people, you begin to realize that you *are* your Higher Self, or as Jean Houston calls it, the "Beloved Self."*

The technique calls for experiencing your self as the Beloved Self until you can no longer distinguish between the two. The result is akin to being reborn as a fully integrated person—a newborn co-creator: *I am that I am.* And as

*Houston, Jean, *The Search for the Beloved: Journeys in Sacred Psychology* (Los Angeles: Jeremy P. Tarcher, Inc., 1987).

a co-creator, you recognize that *what you think manifests.* In our "sleeping state," we often think negative thoughts, make negative statements. Part of waking up is catching ourselves in the act and editing out the negativity before it hardens into abiding thought forms that will manifest in our bodies or in our lives.

Here is a technique to employ whenever you catch yourself saying or hearing something negative or ill-advised. Respond immediately with the words, *I cancel that thought and return it to the plenum from which it came.* By paying attention, we can begin to map the contours of new understanding, and take responsibility for the maps we make.

In 1980, at Mt. Calvary Monastery, Barbara Marx Hubbard had a profound experience following which she dictated without stopping for six months. What follows is an excerpt from what she wrote:

> *You are to become a full demonstration of your potential self, a natural Christ. You are to accelerate your skill of Inner Listening, develop an aura of silence about you like a sound barrier, so you can hear the Voice of God at all times. Learn to let the Inner Voice permeate the walls of the self-conscious mind until the self-conscious mind is wholly absorbed in the God-conscious mind. We are not speaking of years. Time is shortening exponentially as the danger of separation builds and the opportunity for unity accelerates. The critical mass has been reached. The moment of birth approaches. Everyone is being attracted irresistibly to their posts. The mighty design of creation is drawing to it all the builders of the new humanity.* *

*Hubbard, Barbara Marx, *The Manual for Co-Creators* (Irvine, CA: Privately published, 1985), sec. 4, p. 14.

There is a question to ask at this point: If the design of Creation is drawing to it all the builders of humanity, *how do we recognize the real thing from the false?* What are we to make of the ego debris scattered around the landscape by some of the channelers and erratic voices spawned by this culto-genic age?

Wherever the intelligence comes from—whether from *The New York Times* or Lazaris—consider the source by asking: *Do the words resonate within me as deeply true? Do they evoke love and well-being, or fear and pain?* As for the negative messages, rather than taking them as Divine Ordinance, evaluate each one according to these criteria: *Does it foster creativity? Does it permit healing? Does it promote unity?*

The time has come for us to *become* the Oracle, to *be the Person Who Knows.* We must claim oracular consciousness by allowing it to be integrated with the self, by recognizing that the "I that Knows" is within each one of us.

How are we to recognize the presence of this Higher Consciousness? Some people experience it as a feeling of deep relaxation or as a profound sense of relief. This may be accompanied by a sudden onset of clarity that comes when, all at once, you *know* with ease. Often, a rhythmic shift produces a cadence of articulation and beauty far greater than one's normal writing or speaking style. In such moments of clarity, the Oracle *is* the orator.

What is experienced in the oracular mode is both deeper and wiser than the experience of the rational mind, although it doesn't exclude the rational mind. In fact, the rational mind is always delighted by its presence. And when the oracular mode is active in one of us, it can stimulate the same consciousness in others. When that happens, we feel as one. We communicate Oracle to Oracle.

And how will we know that we are following the blueprint for creating the Oracular Individual in ourselves? By our acts. By the way we live our lives. For from each person's increased sensitivity, we will all benefit. The planet will benefit.

Golden Drinking Horn, circa 400 A.D.
Gallehus, South Jutland, Denmark

A TAOIST MEDITATION

*Close your eyes and you will see
  clearly*
*Cease to listen and you will hear
  truth*
Be silent and your heart will sing
*Seek no contact and you will find
  union*
*Be still and you will move forward
  on the the tide of spirit*
*Be gentle and you will need no
  strength*
*Be patient and you will achieve all
  things*
*Be humble and you will remain
  entire.*

*The Björketorp Stone,
åkra, Sweden, circa 600 A.D.*

9

INTERPRETING THE RUNECARDS

The Viking Runes are a mirror for the magic of our Knowing Selves. In time, as you become skilled in their use, you can lay the Runes aside and permit the knowing to arise unfiltered, just as some dowsers use only their bare hands to find water.

—The Book of Runes

he RuneCards are offered to you as a training tool for Intuitive Knowing. There is, however, one thing to remember: *You are not depending on the Oracle to solve your problems for you.* Rather, you are asking to be pointed in the direction where you will find answers for yourself. As you read these Rune interpretations, images and thoughts will come to mind, image-ideas that will provide you with the necessary clues as to what, according to the unconscious, constitutes right action. Working with the Oracle in this way, you will fund a new sense of confidence, a new kind of courage.

There will be times when you have no specific issue in mind and yet still feel inclined to consult the Runes. At such times, a single question, a simple prayer, will always suffice: *Show me what I need to know for my life now.*

When you have been using the RuneCards for a while and are sufficiently conversant with their interpretations, there will come moments when you can tune in to the Runes *without* drawing a card. And as time goes on, you will find yourself more and more able to listen directly to your own Intuitive Wisdom. That is the goal of Sacred Play. That is where the basic training ends.

My intention for the RuneCards is the empowering of the Oracular Individual in service to the Will of the Divine. My hope is that they will support you as you strengthen your practice of the finest art of all, the art of self-change.

Dancing warriors from the Sutton Hoo Helmet,
Suffolk, England, circa 600 A.D.

RUNE
INTERPRETATIONS

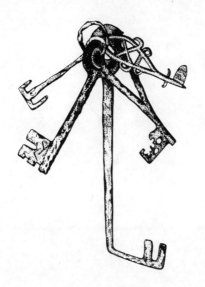

I. THE SELF

MANNAZ

Sun and moon
and your own heart
speak always of that which abides.
In solitude and stillness
know that the journey
begins and ends
with the Self.

The starting point is the self. Its essence is water. Only clarity, willingness to change, is effective now. For from a correct relationship to yourself comes a right relationship to all others and to the Divine.

Remain modest—that is the counsel of *Mannaz.* Regardless of how great may be your merit, be yielding, devoted and moderate, for then your life will have a true direction.

Be in the world but not of it, that is implicit here. And yet do not be closed, narrow, or filled with judgment; rather remain receptive to impulses flowing from the Divine within and without. *Strive to live the ordinary life in a nonordinary way.* Remember at all times what is coming to be and passing away, and focus on that which abides. Nothing less is asked of you now.

This is a time of major growth and rectification and, as a rule, rectification must come before progress. The field is tilled before the seed is planted, the garden is weeded before the flower blooms, and the self must know stillness before it can sing its true song.

This is not a time to seek credit for accomplishments or to focus on results. Rather, be content to do your task for the task's sake. This is more a problem for those whose eyes are always on the goal than for those who have not forgotten how to play and can more easily find themselves in their work. Herein lies the secret of experiencing a *true present*.

If you take the Rune of *The Self* and cut it down the middle, you will see the Rune of *Joy* with its mirror image. There is a subtle caution here against carelessness. The dancing acrobatic energy of balancing is called for now— the Self is required to balance the self. *Nothing in excess* was the second phrase written over the gateway to the temple at Delphi. The first counsel was *Know thyself*.

Reversed: If you feel blocked, do not turn to others, but look inside, in silence, for the enemy of your progress. No matter what area of your life seems to be blocked, stop and consider: You will recognize the outer "enemy" as but a reflection of what you have not, until now, been able or willing to recognize as coming from within.

Above all be humble. Breaking the momentum of past habits is the challenge here: In the life of the Spirit you are always at the beginning.

2. PARTNERSHIP
A Gift

GEBO

I am your beloved,
*   you are my true companion.*
We meet in the circle
*   at the rainbow's center,*
coming together
*   in wholeness.*
That is the gift of freedom.

[X] Drawing this Rune is an indication that partnership in some form is at hand. But you are put on notice not to collapse yourself into that union. For true partnership is only achieved by separate and whole beings who retain their uniqueness even as they unite. This counsel applies at all levels. In love relationships, in business matters, in partnering of every kind, remember to let the winds of Heaven dance between you.

There is another realm of partnership that we are being called to consider. For the path of partnership can lead you to the realization of a still greater union—union with the

Higher Self, union with the Divine. The ultimate gift of this Rune is the realization of the Divine in all things: God always enters into equal partnerships.

Gebo, the Rune of *Partnership,* has no Reverse: It signifies the gift of freedom from which flow all other gifts.

3. SIGNALS

Messenger Rune
The God Loki

ANSUZ

And still the waters rise.
Crossing the deeps,
a messenger brings
the promise of new life unfolding.
Oh Ancient of Days,
may the beauty of your intention
show in our faces.

The keynote here is receiving: messages, signals, gifts. Even a timely warning may be seen as a gift. When the Messenger Rune brings sacred knowledge, one is truly blessed, for the message may be that of a new life unfolding. New lives begin with new connections, surprising linkages that direct us onto new pathways. Take pains now to be especially aware during meetings, visits, chance encounters, particularly with persons wiser than yourself.

The Rune of *Signals* is associated with Loki, the ancient trickster from the pantheon of the Norse gods. He is the *heyeohkah* of the North American Indian, "a mocking shadow of the creator god," the bringer of benefits to humankind. Even scoundrels and arch-thieves can be bearers of wisdom. When you draw this Rune, expect the unexpected: The message is always a call, a call to new life.

Signals is the first of the thirteen Runes that make up the Cycle of Initiation—Runes that focus directly upon the mechanism of self-change—and, as such, addresses your need to integrate unconscious motive with conscious intent. Drawing it tells you that connection with the Divine is at hand. For *Ansuz* asks you to explore the depths, the foundations of life, and to experience the inexhaustible wellspring of the Divine in your nature.

At the same time, you are reminded that you must first draw from the well to nourish and give to yourself. Then there will be more than enough to nourish others. A new sense of family solidarity invests this Rune.

Reversed: You may be concerned over what appears to be failed communication; lack of clarity or awareness either in your past history or in a present situation. You may feel inhibited from accepting what is offered. A sense of futility, of wasted motion, may overwhelm you. Remember, however, that what is happening is timely for your process. If the well is clogged, this is the moment for cleaning out the old. Reversed this Rune is saying: *Consider the uses of adversity.*

4. SEPARATION

Retreat
Inheritance

OTHILA

Paths divide,
*   old skins are shed.*
How skillful the means
*   that free you*
*   to become more truly*
who you are.

This is a time of separating paths. Old skins must be shed, outmoded relationships discarded. When this Rune appears in a spread, a peeling away is called for. Part of the Cycle of Initiation, *Separation* is a Rune of radical severance.

The proper action here is submission and, quite possibly, retreat—knowing how and when to retreat and possessing the firmness of will to carry it out.

Real property is associated with *Othila,* for it is the Rune of acquisition and benefits. However, the benefits you receive, the inheritance, may be derived from something you must give up. Such a surrender can be particularly difficult

133

when that which you are called upon to abandon is an aspect of your behavior or some part of your cultural inheritance. For then you must look closely at what, until now, you have proudly claimed as your birthright. Whether it is your attachment to your position in society, to the work you do or even to your beliefs about your own nature, the separation called for will free you to become more truly who you are.

⟨Ⴘ⟩ **Reversed:** Now is not a time to be bound by old conditioning, old authority. Consider not only what will benefit you but also what will benefit others, and act according to the Light you possess now in your life. Because you may be called upon to undertake a radical departure from old ways, total honesty is required. Otherwise, through negligence or refusal to see clearly, you may cause pain to others and damage to yourself.

Adaptability and skillful means are the qualities to cultivate at this time. Yet you must wait for the universe to act. Receiving this Rune, remember: We do without doing and everything gets done.

5. STRENGTH

Manhood,
Womanhood
The Wild Ox

URUZ

Honor your passage
    into darkness.
        Honor the dying.
The new life holds promises
    unimagined by the old.

The Rune of terminations and new beginnings, drawing *Strength* indicates that the life you have been living has outgrown its form. That form must die so that life energy can be released in a new birth, a new form. This is a Rune of passage and, as such, part of the Cycle of Initiation.

Growth and change, however, may involve a descent into darkness as part of the cycle of perpetual renewal. As in Nature, the progression consists of five parts: death, decay, fertilization, gestation, rebirth. Events occurring now may well prompt you to undergo a death within yourself. Since self-change is never coerced—we are always free to resist—remain mindful that the new form, the new life, is always greater than the old.

Prepare, then, for opportunity disguised as loss. This could involve the loss of something or even someone with whom you have an intense emotional bond, and through whom you are living a part of your life, a part that must now be retrieved so you can live it out for yourself. In some way, that bond is being severed, a relationship radically changed, a way of life coming to an end. Seek among the ashes and discover a new perspective and new strength.

The original symbol for *Uruz* was the aurochs, a wild ox. When the wild ox was domesticated—a nearly impossible task—it could transport heavy loads. Learn to adapt yourself to the demands of such a creative time. Firm principles attach to this Rune, and at the same time humility is called for, since in order to rule you must learn how to serve. The Rune of *Strength* puts you on notice that your soul and the universe support the new growth.

Reversed: Without ears to hear and eyes to see, you may fail to take advantage of the moment. The result could well be an opportunity missed or the weakening of your position. It may seem that your own strength is being used against you.

For some, *Strength Reversed* will serve to alert, offering clues in the form of minor failures and disappointments. For others, those more deeply unaware, it may provide a hard jolt. Reversed, this Rune calls for serious thought about the quality of your relationship to your Self.

But take heart. Consider the constant cycling of death and rebirth, the endless going and return. Everything we experience has a beginning, a middle, an end, and is followed by a new beginning. Therefore do not draw back from the passage into darkness. When in deep water, become a diver.

6. INITIATION

Something Hidden
A Secret Matter

PERTH

Rise and soar on wings
of renewed spirit.
What looked familiar before
will seem strange,
what seemed strange, familiar.

 A hieratic or mystery Rune, *Initiation* points to that
which is beyond our frail manipulative powers. *Perth* is on
the side of Heaven, the Unknowable, and has associations
with the phoenix, that mystical bird which consumes itself
in the fire and then rises from its own ashes. Its ways are
secret and hidden.

Powerful forces of change are at work here. Yet what is
achieved is not easily or readily shared. After all, becoming
whole, the means of it, is a profound secret.

On the side of the earthly or mundane, there may well
be surprises; unexpected gains are not unlikely. On the side
of human nature, this Rune is symbolized by the flight of

the eagle. Soaring flight, free from entanglement, lifting yourself above the endless ebb and flow of ordinary life to acquire broader vision—all this is indicated here. This is the Rune of questing.

Another of the Cycle Runes, *Initiation* is concerned with the deepest stratum of being, with the bedrock on which your destiny is founded. *Nothing external matters here except as it shows you its inner reflection.* For some, drawing *Perth* means experiencing a psychic death. If need be, let go of everything, no exceptions, no exclusions. Nothing less than renewal of the Spirit is at stake.

Reversed: A counsel against expecting too much, or expecting in the ordinary way, for the old way has come to an end: You simply cannot repeat the old and not suffer. Call in your scattered energies, concentrate on your own life at this moment, your own requirements for growth. More important, *Initiation* counsels you neither to focus on outcomes, nor to bind yourself with the memory of past achievements. In doing so, you rob yourself of a true present, which is the only time in which self-change can be realized.

You may feel overwhelmed with exhaustion from meeting obstruction upon obstruction in your passage. Yet you always have a choice: You can see all this apparent negativity as bad luck, or you can recognize it as an obstacle course, a challenge specific to the initiation you are presently undergoing. Then each setback, each humiliation, becomes a test of character. When your inner being is shifting and reforming on a deep level, patience, constancy and perseverance are called for. So stay centered, see the humor, and keep your Faith firm.

7. CONSTRAINT

Necessity
Pain

NAUTHIZ

Follow the glistening dew drops
to the center of the web.
Limitations define us,
Ordeals temper us.
See the Great Teacher
behind every disguise.

The necessity of dealing with severe constraint is the lesson of this Rune. The positive aspects of *Nauthiz* represent the limitations we directly cause ourselves. Its negative side attracts limitations from those around us. Both can be equally difficult to handle.

The role of *Constraint* is to identify our "shadow," our dark or repressed side, areas where growth has been stunted, resulting in weaknesses that we project onto others. *Don't take this world personally,* this Rune is saying. Work with the shadow, examine what inside you magnetizes misfortune into your life. When at last you can look upon

Nauthiz with a smile, you will recognize the troubles, denials and setbacks of life as your teachers, guides and allies.

The need for restraint is unquestionable here. Drawing this Rune indicates that there will be holdups, reasons to reconsider your plans carefully. There is work to be done on your self. So take it on with good will and show perseverance.

This is a time to pay off old debts, to restore, if not harmony, at least balance. So mend, restore, redress: When fishermen can't go to sea they repair nets. Let the constraints of this time serve you in righting your relationship to your Self. Be mindful that rectification comes before progress. And once again, consider the uses of adversity.

Reversed: As part of the Cycle of Initiation, *Constraint* is the great teacher disguised as the bringer of pain and limitation. It has been said that only at the point of greatest darkness do we become aware of the Light within us by which we come to recognize the true creative power of the self.

When something within us is disowned, that which is disowned wreaks havoc. A cleansing is required here; in undertaking it you fund a will and strengthen character. Begin with what is most difficult and proceed to that which is easy. Or, conversely, begin with what is easy and proceed to that which is most difficult. Either way, remember that "suffering," in its original sense, merely meant "undergoing." Thus you may be required to undergo the dark side of your passage and bring it into the Light. Controlling your anger, restraining your impulses, keeping your faith firm—all this is at issue here. Modesty and good temper are essential at such a time.

8. FERTILITY

New Beginnings
The Hero-God Ing

INGUZ

A butterfly emerges
still moist from the cocoon.
This is how new life comes,
softly, secretly,
among the green shoots.

◊ This Rune is akin to the moon, the intuitive part of our nature, with its urge toward harmonizing and adjusting in the sphere of personal relationships. *Fertility* embodies the need to share, the yearning to be desired, a search after similarities.

The completion of beginnings is what *Inguz* requires. It may mark a time of joyous deliverance, of new life, a new path. A Rune of great power, drawing it means that you now have the strength to achieve completion, resolution, from which comes a new beginning. Above all, completion is crucial here. It may be timely that you complete some project now; if so, make that your first priority. Perhaps a difficult state of mind can be resolved, clarified, turned around. Drawing this Rune indicates that you must first fertilize the ground for your own deliverance.

All things change and we cannot live permanently amid obstructions. The Rune of *Fertility* signals your emergence from a closed chrysalis state. As you resolve and clear away the old, you will experience a release from tension and uncertainty.

You may be required to free yourself from a rut, habit or relationship; from some deep cultural or behavioral pattern, some activity that was quite proper to the self you are leaving behind. The period at or just before birth is often a dangerous one. Movement involves danger, yet movement that is timely leads out of danger. Now it is time to enter the delivery room.

Another of the Cycle Runes, *Fertility* counsels preparation. Being centered and grounded, freeing yourself from all unwanted influences, and seeing the humor, you are indeed prepared to open yourself to the Will of Heaven and can await your deliverance with calm certainty.

9. DEFENSE

Avertive Powers
Yew Tree

EIHWAZ

Red berries
gathered from the labyrinth
will sustain you.
As you meet
obstacles on your way,
call each one
Teacher and Friend.

 As we are tested we fund the power to avert blockage and defeat. At the same time, we develop in ourselves an aversion to the conduct that creates stress in our lives.

If there appears to be an obstacle in your path, consider that even a delay may prove beneficial. Do not be overly eager to press forward, for this is not a situation in which you can make your influence felt. Patience is the counsel *Eihwaz* offers: nothing hectic, no acting needy, or lusting after a desired outcome. This Rune speaks to the difficulties that arise at the beginning of new life. Often it announces a time of waiting—for a spring to fill up with water, for fruit to ripen on the bough.

Perseverance and foresight are called for here. The ability to foresee consequences before you act is a mark of the profound person. Avert anticipated difficulties through right action. For even more than we are *doers,* we are *deciders.* And once the decision is clear, the doing becomes effortless.

Receiving the Rune of *Defense* you are put on notice that, through inconvenience and discomfort, growth is promoted. For as the wood of the yew tree becomes the bow of the Spiritual Warrior, so each obstacle on your path can become the gateway to a new life unfolding.

This may well be a trying time; certainly it is a meaningful one. So set your house in order, tend to business, be clear, and wait on the Will of Heaven.

10. PROTECTION

Sedge or Rushes
The Elk

ALGIZ

The dunes shift
and shift forever,
>*feather grass restless*
>>*in the wind.*
Cool your emotions.
>*Follow your path.*
That is your protection.

Control of the emotions is at issue here. During times of transition, shifts in life course, and accelerated self-change, it is important not to collapse into your emotions— the highs as well as the lows. New opportunities and challenges are typical of this Rune. And with them may come trespasses and unwanted influences.

Protection serves as a mirror for the Spiritual Warrior, the one whose battle is always with the self. The protection of the Warrior is like the warning rustle of the sedge grass or like the curved horns of the elk, for both serve to keep open space around you. Remain mindful that timely action and correct conduct are the only true protection. If you find yourself feeling pain, observe the pain, stay with it. Don't try to pull down the veil and escape from life by denying what is happening. You *will* progress; knowing that is your protection.

Reversed: Be thoughtful about your health. Do not add to the burdens others are carrying. Look carefully at the associations you form at this time. If you see fit to become involved with people who are using you, remain conscious of that fact and take responsibility for your own position; then you can only benefit. Regardless of whether your enterprise prospers or suffers, do not be concerned: You may not win, but you will never lose, for you will always learn from what takes place. Temperance and courtesy are the sinews of this Rune's protective powers.

II. POSSESSIONS

Nourishment
Cattle

FEHU

Everything speaks of choice.
The true kernel lies
hidden in the soul.
Be devout in your attention
and you will be nourished.

F *Possessions* is a Rune of fulfillment: ambition satisfied, love fulfilled, rewards received. It promises nourishment, from the most worldly to the sacred and the Divine. Moreover, if the ancient hermetic principle *As above so below* holds true, then we are also here to nourish God.

This Rune calls for a deep probing of the meaning of profit and gain in your life. Look with care to know whether it is wealth and possessions you require for your well-being, or rather self-rule and the growth of a will.

Another concern of *Fehu* is with conserving what has already been gained. It urges vigilance and continual mindfulness, especially in times of good fortune, for it is then that we are likely to collapse ourselves into our success on the one hand, or to behave recklessly on the other. Enjoy your good fortune and remember to share it: The mark of the well-nourished self is the ability and willingness to nourish others.

Reversed: There may be considerable frustration in your life if you draw *Possessions Reversed*—a wide range of dispossessions reaching from the trivial to the severe. You fall short in your efforts, you reach out and miss, you watch helplessly while what you've gained dwindles away. Observe what is happening. Examine these events from an open perspective and ask, "What lesson do I need to learn from this in my life?"

Even if there is occasion for joy, do not let yourself be seduced into mindless joyousness. Reversed, this Rune indicates that doubtful situations are abundant and come in many forms and guises. You are being put in touch with the shadow side of possessions. Yet all this is part of coming to be and passing away, and not that which abides. In dealing with the shadow side of *Fehu,* you have an opportunity to recognize where your true nourishment lies.

12. JOY

Light

WUNJO

The storm clouds
        have parted
                and Heaven's breath
glows on the water.
        Knowing such beauty,
shall I not say
        that I am truly blessed?

This Rune is a fruit-bearing branch. The term of travail is ended and you have come to yourself in some regard. The shift that was due has occurred and now you can freely receive *Joy*'s blessings, whether they be in material gain, in your emotional life or in a heightened sense of your own well-being. This is an alchemical moment in which understanding is transmuted from knowledge. The knowledge itself was a necessary but not sufficient condition; now you can rejoice, having been carried across the gap by the Will of Heaven.

Joyousness accompanies new energy, energy blocked

before now. Light pierces the clouds and touches the waters just as something lovely emerges from the depths: The soul is illuminated from within, at the meeting place of Heaven and Earth, the meeting of the waters.

There is a new clarity which may call for you to renounce existing plans, ambitions, goals. It is proper and timely for you to do so, for *Wunjo* is a Rune of restoration, of the self properly aligned to the Self.

Reversed: Things are slow in coming to fruition. The process of birth is long and arduous, and fears arise for the safety of the "child" within. A crisis, a difficult passage—even if brief—is at hand. Consideration and deliberation are called for. Ask yourself whether you possess the virtues of seriousness, sincerity, and emptiness; to possess them is to have tranquility, which is the ground for clarity, patience and perseverance.

Seen in its true light, everything is a test. And so, focused in the present, sincere toward others and trusting in your process, know that you cannot fail.

In times of crisis, *Joy Reversed* is a useful meditation.

13. HARVEST

Fertile Season
One Year

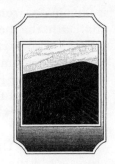

JERA

The first green shoots
    sprout from turned earth.
Patience, patience,
    my beloved.
In your season
    you will know
        the harvest of the self.

A Rune of beneficial outcomes, *Harvest* applies to any activity or endeavor to which you are committed. Be aware, however, that no quick results can be expected. A span of time is always involved; hence the key words "one year," symbolizing a full cycle before the reaping, the harvest or deliverance.

You have prepared the ground and planted the seed. Now you must cultivate with care. To those whose labor has a long season, a long coming to term, *Jera* offers encouragement of success. Know that the outcome is in the keeping of Providence and continue to persevere.

Remember the old story about the farmer who was so eager to assist his crops that he went out at night and tugged on the new shoots. There is no way to push the river; equally, you cannot hasten the harvest. Be mindful that patience is essential for the recognition and acceptance of your own process which, in its season, leads to the harvest of the self.

14. OPENING

Fire
Torch

KANO

Fire is Heaven's light
in its palest hue.
That fiery branch
burning at the heart's center
claims its kinship
with the sun.
What hid itself in shadows
is clear to me now.

This is the Rune of opening, renewed clarity, dispelling the darkness that has been shrouding some part of your life. You are free now to receive and to know the joy of nonattached giving.

Opening is the Rune for the morning of activities, for seriousness, clear intent and concentration, all of which are essential at the beginning of any endeavor. The protection offered by *Kano* is this: The more Light you have, the better you can see what is trivial and outmoded in your own conditioning.

In relationships, there can now be a mutual opening up. You may be called to serve as the trigger, the timekeeper, through your awareness that the Light of understanding is once again available to you both.

Recognize that while on the one hand you are limited and dependent, on the other you exist at the perfect center where the harmonious and beneficent forces of the universe merge and radiate. You *are* that center.

Simply put, if you have been operating in the dark, there is now enough light to see that the patient on the operating table is yourself.

Reversed: Expect a darkening of the light in some situation or relationship. A friendship may be dying, a partnership, a marriage or some aspect of yourself that is no longer appropriate to the person you are now becoming. Receiving this Rune puts you on notice that failure to face up to the death consciously would constitute a loss of opportunity. *Opening* is one of the Cycle Runes. Reversed, it points to the death of a way of life that is no longer valid.

Opening Reversed calls for giving up gladly the old, and being prepared to live for a time empty. It calls for developing inner stability; not being seduced by the momentum of old ways while waiting for the new to become illuminated in its proper time.

15. WARRIOR
The Sky God Tiw

TEIWAZ

Undertake your passage
in trust and innocence,
for such is the Warrior Way.
And at the end,
send heavenward
the burning arrows
of your perfect faith.

⬆ This is the Rune of the Spiritual Warrior. Always the battle for the Spiritual Warrior is with the self. Funding a will through action yet unattached to outcomes, able to be radically alone, remaining mindful that all you can really do is stay out of your own way and let the Will of Heaven flow through you—these are among the hallmarks of the Spiritual Warrior.

Embodied in this Rune is the energy of discrimination, the swordlike quality that enables you to cut away the old, the dead, the extraneous. And yet, with the *Warrior* comes certain knowledge that the universe always has the first move. Patience is the virtue of this Rune, and it recalls the words of St. Augustine that *the reward of patience is patience.*

Here, you are asked to look within, to delve down to the foundations of life itself. Only in so doing can you hope to satisfy the deepest needs of your nature and tap into your most profound resources. The molding of character is at issue when *Teiwaz* appears in a spread.

Associated with this Rune are the sun, masculine energy, the active principle. The urge toward conquest is prominent here, especially self-conquest, which is a lifelong pursuit and calls for awareness, single-mindedness and the willingness to undergo your passage with compassion and in total trust.

In issues of relationship, devotion to a cause, an idea or a path of conduct, the *Warrior* Rune counsels perseverance, although at times the kind of perseverance required is patience.

Teiwaz is a Rune of courage and dedication. In ancient times it was this glyph that warriors painted on their shields before battle. Now, the same symbol strengthens your resolve in the struggle of the Self with the self.

⬇ **Reversed:** The danger is that through hasty or ill-timed action, life force leaks out or is spilled away. If an association is short-lived, do not grieve, but know that it has fulfilled its span. Matters of trust and confidence are at issue here, and with them the authenticity of your way of going through the world.

Reversed, *Teiwaz* calls for examining your motives. Is it self-conquest with which you are concerned, or are you trying to dominate another? Are you lusting after outcomes, or are you focused on the task for its own sake?

You will find the answers within yourself, not in outside advice. When you consult the Runes, you are consulting the Self, which is the action appropriate to a Spiritual Warrior.

16. GROWTH

Rebirth
A Birch Tree

BERKANA

We grow as the tree grows,
putting out new leaves in Spring.
And through it all,
the soul remains hidden,
adding ring upon ring upon ring.

Another of the Cycle Runes, *Growth* denotes a form of fertility that fosters growth both symbolically and actually. The growth may occur in affairs of the world, family matters, one's relationship to one's self or to the Divine.

A Rune that leads to blossoming and ripening, *Berkana* is concerned with the flow of beings into their new forms. Its action is gentle, penetrating and pervasive.

What is called for here is going into things deeply, with care and awareness. First disperse resistance, then accomplish the work. For this to happen, your will must be clear and controlled, your motives correct. Any dark corners should be cleansed; this must be carried out diligently, and sometimes with expert help. Modesty, patience, fairness and generosity are called for here. Once resistance is dispersed and rectification carried out and seen to hold firm, then, through steadfastness and right attitude, the blossoming can occur.

Reversed: Events or, more likely, aspects of character interfere with the growth of new life. You may feel dismay at failing to take right action. But rather than dismay, what is called for is diligence. You may be required to fertilize the ground again, but through correct preparation, growth is assured.

Examine what has occurred, your role in it, your needs, the needs of others. Are you placing your *wants* before the *needs* of others? Strip away until you can identify the obstacles to growth in this situation. Then, penetrating gently, imitate the wind.

17. MOVEMENT

Progress
A Horse

EHWAZ

The warrior ship
plows the waves,
yet no hand grasps the tiller,
none draws an oar.
Oh mariner,
surrender to the mystery.
All else follows.

[M] *Ehwaz* is a Rune of transit and transition; of physical shifts, new dwelling places, new attitudes or new life. It also signifies movement in the sense of improving or bettering any situation.

There is about this Rune a sense of gradual development and steady progress, with the accompanying notion of slow growth through numerous shifts and changes. This could apply to the growth of a business or to the development of an idea. A relationship may need to undergo changes if it is to maintain growth and life. Moral effort and steadfastness are called for when you draw *Movement,* another of the Cycle Runes. Let it be said this way: *As I cultivate my own nature, all else follows.*

This Rune's symbol is the horse, and it signifies the bond between horse and rider. Bronze Age artifacts show a horse drawing the sun across the sky. Here, *Ehwaz* is saying, you have progressed far enough to feel a measure of safety in your position. It is time to turn again and face the future reassured, prepared to share the good fortune that comes. The sharing is significant since it relates to the sun's power to foster life and illuminate all things with its light.

Reversed: Movement that appears to block. Be certain that what you are doing—or not doing—is timely. You have simply to recognize that not all opportunities are appropriate, that not all possibilities are open to you. The opportunity at hand may be precisely to avoid action. If you are feeling at a loss, unclear about the need to act, consider what is timely to your nature, and remember: *What is yours will come to you.*

18. FLOW

Water
That Which Conducts

LAGUZ

Between Movement
*   and Disruption*
*   comes a perfect moment*
when all things sing together—
sky, sea, sand, earth, blood.
Their song is called Flowering.

⌐ Unseen powers are active here, powers that nourish, shape and connect. The attributes of this Rune are water, fluidity, the ebb and flow of emotions, of vocations and relationships. *Laguz* supports your desire to immerse yourself in the experience of living without having to evaluate or understand. It speaks to the satisfaction of emotional needs, to the awakening of the intuitive or lunar side of your nature. For while the sun strives for differentiation, the moon draws us toward union and merging.

This Rune often signals a time for cleansing: for revaluing, reorganizing, realigning. A Rune of deep knowing,

Laguz may call you to study spiritual matters in readiness for self-transformation. Success now lies in contacting your Intuitive Knowing, in attuning to your own rhythms. A Rune of the self relating rightly to the Self, *Flow* signifies what alchemists called the *conjunctio,* or sacred marriage. In fairy tales, it is the end where the hero and heroine live happily ever after.

Reversed: A warning against overreach, excessive striving; a counsel against trying to exceed your own strength or operate beyond the power you have funded to date in your life.

Flow Reversed often indicates a failure to draw upon the wisdom of instinct. As a result, the intuitive side of your nature may be languishing, leaving you out of balance. What is called for now is to go within, to honor the receptive side of your Warrior Nature.

19. DISRUPTION

Elemental Power
Hail

HAGALAZ

The moon is hidden,
thunder strikes.
How can you sleep
when your very bed
calls in the lightning?
Look around you.
Nothing is the same.

 Change, freedom, invention and liberation are all attributes of this Rune. Drawing it indicates a pressing need within the psyche to break free from constricting identification with material reality and to experience the world of archetypal mind.

The Rune of elemental disruption, of events that seem to be totally beyond your control, *Hagalaz* has only an upright position, and yet it always operates through reversal. When you draw this Rune, expect disruption, for it is the Great Awakener, although the form the awakening takes may vary. Perhaps you will experience a gradual feeling of coming to your senses, as though you were emerging from a long sleep. Then again, the onset of power may be such as to rip away the fabric of what you previously knew as your reality, your security, your understanding of yourself, your work, relationships or beliefs.

Be aware, however, that what operates here is not ultimately an outside force, not a situation of you at the mercy of external events. Your own nature is creating what is happening, and you are not without power. The inner strength you have funded until now in your life is your support and guide at a time when everything you've taken for granted is being challenged.

Receiving this Rune puts you on notice: You may sustain loss or damage—a relationship fails, plans go awry, a source of supply dries up. But do not be dismayed. You are forewarned and, therefore, encouraged to understand and accept what occurs as necessary for your growth.

The more severe the disruption in your life, the more significant and timely the requirements for your growth. Another of the Cycle Runes, the term *radical discontinuity* best describes the action of *Hagalaz* at its most forceful. The universe and your own soul are demanding that you do, indeed, grow.

20. JOURNEY

Communication
Union, Reunion

RAIDO

The path grows steeper now,
the clouds lie far below.
I climb, no longer alone,
and yet no longer burdened
by what was left behind.
My heart is filled with gratitude.

 This Rune is concerned with communication, with the attunement of something that has two sides, two elements, and with the ultimate reunion that comes at the end of the journey, when what is above and what is below are united and of one mind.

Inner worth mounts here, and at such a time you must remember that you are not intended to rely entirely upon your own power, but rather to ask what constitutes right action. Ask through prayer, through addressing your own knowing, the Witness Self, the Teacher Within. Not intent on movement, be content to wait; while you wait, keep on removing resistances. As the obstructions give way, all remorse arising from "trying to make it happen" disappears.

The journey is toward self-healing, self-change and union. You are concerned here with nothing less than unobstructed, perfect union. But the union of Heaven and Earth cannot be forced. Regulate any excesses in your life. Material advantages must not weigh heavily on this journey of the self toward the Self. Stand apart even from like-minded others; the notion of strength in numbers does not apply here, for this part of the journey cannot be shared.

Another of the Cycle Runes, *Raido* represents the soul's journey and has within it the element of Joy, for the end is in sight. No longer burdened by what you've left behind, Heaven above you and the Earth below you unite within you to support you on your way. A simple prayer for the soul's journey is:

I will to will Thy Will.

⟨ℝ⟩ **Reversed:** Receiving this Rune Reversed puts you on notice to be particularly attentive to personal relationships. At this time, ruptures are more likely than reconciliations. Effort will be required to keep your good humor. Whatever happens, how you respond is up to you.

The requirements of your process may totally disrupt what you had intended. Hoped-for outcomes may elude you. And yet what you regard as detours, inconveniences, disruptions, obstacles and even failures and deaths will actually be *rerouting opportunities,* with union and reunion as the only abiding destinations.

21. GATEWAY

Place of Non-Action
The God Thor

THURISAZ

Be a lover of gateways.
  Approach them softly.
For once you pass through
  there will be changes
and much that you
  will gladly lay aside.

ᚦ With a gateway for its symbol, this Rune indicates that there is work to be done both inside and outside yourself. *Gateway* represents the frontier between Heaven and the mundane. Arriving here is a recognition of your readiness to contact the numinous, the Divine, to illuminate your experience so that its meaning shines through its form.

Thurisaz is a Rune of non-action. Thus, the gateway is not to be approached and passed through without contemplation. Here you are being confronted with a clear reflection of what is hidden in yourself, what must be exposed and examined before successful action can be undertaken. This

Rune strengthens your ability to wait. Now is not a time to make decisions. Deep transformational forces are at work in this next-to-last of the Cycle Runes.

Visualize yourself standing before a gateway on a hilltop. Your entire life lies out behind you and below. Before you step through, pause and review the past: the learning and the joys, the victories and the sorrows—everything it took to bring you here. Observe it all, bless it all, release it all. For in letting go of the past you reclaim your power.

Step through the gateway now.

◁ **Reversed:** A quickening of your development is indicated here. And yet even when the growth process accelerates, you will have reason to halt along the way, to reconsider the old, to integrate the new. Take advantage of these halts.

If you are undergoing difficulties, remember: The quality of your passage depends upon your attitude and upon the clarity of your intention. Be certain that you are not suffering over your suffering.

Drawing *Gateway Reversed* demands contemplation on your part. Hasty decisions at this time may cause regrets, for the probability is that you will act from weakness, deceive yourself about your motives and create new problems more severe than those you are attempting to resolve. Impulses must be tempered by thought for correct procedure. *Do not attempt to go beyond where you haven't yet begun.* Be still, collect yourself, and wait on the Will of Heaven.

22. BREAKTHROUGH

Transformation
Day

DAGAZ

Down the cathedral aisles
of deep and ancient forests
  bursts the morning fire.
Take heart, my Beloved.
What is Divine
  cannot be separated
from its Source.

 Here is the final Rune belonging to the Cycle of Initiation. Drawing *Dagaz* often signals a major shift or breakthrough in the process of self-change, a complete transformation in attitude—a 180-degree turn. For some, the transition is so radical that they no longer continue to live the ordinary life in the ordinary way.

Because the timing is right, the outcome is assured although not, from the present vantage point, predictable. In each life there comes at least one moment which, if recognized and seized, transforms the course of that life forever.

Rely, therefore, on radical trust, even though the moment may call for you to leap empty-handed into the void. With this Rune your Warrior Nature reveals itself.

If *Breakthrough* is followed by *The Blank Rune,* the magnitude of the transformation might be so total as to portend a death, the successful conclusion of your passage.

A major period of achievement and prosperity is often introduced by this Rune. The darkness is behind you; daylight has come. However, as always, you are reminded not to collapse yourself into the future or to behave recklessly in your new situation. Considerable hard work can be involved in a time of transformation. Undertake to do it joyfully.

23. STANDSTILL

That Which Impedes
Ice

ISA

Praise Winter.
  Gather snowdrops.
Listen for your name
       on the chill wind
       and bless the seeds
       waiting in the darkness
for the call of Spring.

 Drawing *Standstill* often indicates that the winter of the spiritual life is upon you. You may find yourself entangled in a situation to whose implications you are, in effect, blind. You may be powerless to do anything except submit, surrender, even sacrifice some long-cherished desire. But be patient, for this is the period of gestation that precedes a rebirth.

Positive accomplishment is unlikely now. There is a freeze on useful activity, all your plans are on hold. You may be experiencing an unaccustomed drain on your energy and wonder why: A chill wind is reaching you over the ice floes of old, outmoded habits.

Trying to hold on can result in shallowness of feeling, a sense of being out of touch with life. Seek to discover what it is you are holding on to that keeps this condition in effect, and let it go. Shed, release, cleanse away the old. That will bring on the thaw.

Usually *Isa* requires a sacrifice of the personal, the "I". And yet there is no reason for anxiety. Submit and be still, for what you are experiencing is not necessarily the result of your actions or habits, but of the conditions of the time against which you can do nothing. What has been full must empty; what has increased must decrease. This is the way of Heaven and Earth. To surrender is to display courage and wisdom.

At such a time, you cannot hope to rely on help or friendly support. In your isolation, exercise caution and do not stubbornly persist in attempting to work your will. Remain mindful that the seed of the new is present in the shell of the old, the seed of unrealized potential, the seed of the good. Trust your own process, and watch for signs of spring.

24. WHOLENESS

Life Forces
The Sun's Energy

SOWELU

Where is the boundary
between Earth and Heaven?
After all, it is Love
that loves through us,
is it not?

 This Rune stands for wholeness, that which your nature requires. It embodies the impulse toward self-realization and indicates the path you must follow, not from ulterior motives but from the core of your individuality.

Seeking after wholeness is the Spiritual Warrior's quest. And yet what you are striving to become in actuality is what you, by nature, already are. You must become conscious of your essence and bring it into form, express it in a creative way. A Rune of great power, making life force available to you, *Sowelu* marks a time for regeneration right down to the cellular level.

Although this Rune has no Reversed position, there is reason for caution. You may see fit to withdraw, to retreat in the face of a pressing situation, especially if events or people are demanding that you expend your energy now. Know that such a retreat is a retreat in strength, and that it can indicate the need for a voyage inward for centering, for balance. Timely retreat is among the skills of the Spiritual Warrior.

At the same time, for some this Rune counsels opening yourself up, letting the Light into a part of your life that has been secret, shut away. To accomplish this may call for profound recognitions, for admitting to yourself something that you have long denied.

There is a prayer, known as the *Gayatri,* which embodies the spirit of *Wholeness.* Address the sun in this fashion:

> *You, who are the source of all power,*
> *Whose rays illuminate the whole world,*
> *Illuminate also my heart*
> *So that it too can do Your Work.*

While reciting the Gayatri, visualize the sun's rays streaming forth into the world, entering your heart, then streaming out from your heart's center and back into the world. This a powerful and life-enhancing prayer.

There is a caution here not to give yourself airs. Even in a time of bountiful energy, you are required to face and vanquish your refusal to let right action flow through you. Nourish this capacity, for it is a mark of true humility.

Practice the art of doing without doing: Aim yourself truly, then maintain your aim without manipulative effort. Meditate on Christ's words: *I can of mine own self do nothing.*

For by our own power we do nothing. Even in loving, it is Love that loves through us. This way of thinking and being integrates new energies and permits you to flow into Wholeness, which is the ultimate goal of the Spiritual Warrior.

25. THE UNKNOWABLE

THE BLANK RUNE

Total trust,
    surrender,
    relinquishing control—
all this is only words.
    Look into the night sky.
    Tell me what you see.

Blank is the end, blank the beginning. This is the Rune of total trust and should be taken as exciting evidence of your most immediate contact with your own true destiny which, time and again, rises like the phoenix from the ashes of what we call fate.

Drawing *The Unknowable* can portend a death. But that death is usually symbolic, and may relate to any part of your life as you are living it now. *Relinquishing control is the ultimate challenge for the Spiritual Warrior.*

Here the Unknowable informs you that it is in motion in your life. In that blankness is held undiluted potential. At the same time both pregnant and empty, it comprehends the totality of being, all that is to be actualized. And if, indeed, there are "matters hidden by the gods," you need only remember: What beckons is the creative power of the unknown.

The Blank Rune may bring to the surface your deepest fears: Will I fail? Will I be abandoned? Will it all be taken away? And yet your highest good, your truest possibilities and all your fertile dreams are held within that blankness.

Willingness and permitting are what this Rune requires, for how can you exercise control over what is not yet in form? *The Blank Rune* often calls for no less an act of courage than the empty-handed leap into the void. Drawing it is a direct test of Faith.

The Unknowable represents the path of *karma*—the sum total of your actions and of their consequences. At the same time, this Rune teaches that the very debts of old karma shift and evolve as you shift and evolve. *Nothing is predestined.*

Whenever you draw this Rune, take heart: Know that the work of self-change is progressing in your life.

ENVOI

When God is present,
there is no reason
to speak the Holy Name.

—My Grandfather

BIBLIOGRAPHY

The following bibliography, while including few primary sources and not exhaustive, is intended for those who wish to go more deeply into runic and related studies. Certain books listed (such as Loyn, Flowers, Elliott, Page and others) contain more extensive bibliographies.

Anonymous. *Meditations on the Tarot: A Journey Into Christian Hermeticism.* Amity, New York: Amity House, 1985.

Badenoch, Lindsay. *The Daughter of the Runes.* London: Arkana, 1988.

Bates, Brian. *The Way of Wyrd.* London: Century Publishing, 1983.

Beaman, Donald G. *Rune Ryngs.* Boston: Privately Printed, 1988.

Blum, Ralph. *The Book of Runes.* New York: St. Martin's Press, 1983.

———. *Rune Play.* New York: Oracle Books, St. Martin's Press, 1985.

Bonner, W. "Survivals of Paganism in Anglo-Saxon England." *Transactions of the Birmingham Archaeological Society,* vol. 56, 1932.

Branston, B. *The Lost Gods of England.* London: Thames and Hudson, 1957.

Chadwick, H. M. *The Cult of Othin.* London: Clay and Sons, 1899.

Clark, Anthony. *The Aquarian Rune Pack.* Wellingborough, England: Aquarian, 1987.

Dickens, Bruce. *Runic and Heroic Poems of the Old Teutonic Peoples.* Cambridge: Cambridge University Press, 1915.

———. "English Names and Old English Heathenism." *Essays and Studies,* vol. 19, 1934.

———. "Runic Rings and Old English Charms." *Archiv Stud. neuren Sprachen,* vol. 167, 1935.

———. "A System of Transliteration for Old English Runic Inscriptions." *Leeds Studies in English,* vol. 1, 1932.

Dolphin, Deon. *Rune Magic: The Celtic Runes as a Tool for Personal Transformation.* North Hollywood, California: Newcastle, 1987.

Eddison, E. R. *Egil's Saga.* Cambridge: Cambridge University Press, 1930.

Elliot, Ralph W. V. *Runes: An Introduction.* Manchester: Manchester University Press, 1959 (revised 1989).

———. "Runes, Yews, and Magic." *Speculum,* vol. 32, 1957.

Ellis, Hilda R. *The Road to Hel.* Cambridge: Cambridge University Press, 1943.

Ellis Davidson, Hilda R. *Gods and Myths of Northern Europe.* London: Penguin, 1946.

Flowers, Stephen E. *Runes and Magic: Magical Formulaic Elements in the Older Runic Tradition.* New York: Peter Lang, 1986.

Franz, Marie-Louise von. *On Divination and Synchronicity: The Psychology of Meaningful Chance.* Toronto: Inner City Books, 1980.

Graham-Campbell, James. *Viking Artifacts, A Select Catalogue.* London: British Museum Publications Limited, 1980.

Grattan, J. H. G., and Singer, S. *Anglo-Saxon Magic and Medicine.* London: 1952.

Halsall, Maureen. *The Old English Rune Poem: A Critical Edition* (McMaster Old English Studies and Texts 2). Toronto: University of Toronto Press, 1981.

Haugen, Einar. *The Scandinavian Languages.* Cambridge, Massachusetts: Harvard University Press, 1976.

Hermannsson, H. *Catalogue of Runic Literature*—Part of the Icelandic Collection Bequeathed by Willard Fiske. Cornell University Library.

Hollander, Lee M. *The Poetic Edda.* Austin: University of Texas Press, 1964.

Holmzvist, Wilhem. *Swedish Vikings on Helgo and Birka.* Stockholm: Swedish Booksellers Association, 1979.

Howard, Michael. *The Magic of the Runes.* New York: Samuel Weiser, 1980.

————. *The Runes and Other Magical Alphabets.* Wellingborough, Northants, England: Aquarian Press, 1978.

Jansson, Sven B. F. *The Runes of Sweden.* Translated by Peter Foote. London: Phoenix House, 1962.

Jones, Gwyn. *History of the Vikings.* London: Oxford University Press, 1968.

Jung, Carl G. *Synchronicity: An Acausal Connecting Principle.* Princeton: Princeton University Press, 1973.

Knoop, Douglas, and Jones, G. P. *The Mediaeval Mason.* Manchester, England: Manchester University Press, 1967.

Koestler, Arthur. *The Roots of Coincidence.* London: Hutchinson & Co. Ltd., 1972.

Krause, Wolfgang. *Was Mann in Runen Ritzte.* Halle, Germany: M. Niemeyer, 1935.

Line, David and Julia. *Fortune-Telling by Runes.* Wellingborough, England: Aquarian Press, 1984.

Lowe, Michael and Blacker, Carmen. *Oracles and Divination.* Boulder, Colorado: Shambhala, 1981.

Loyn, H. R. *The Vikings in Britain.* New York: St. Martin's Press, 1977.

Magnusson, Magnus. *Hammer of the North.* London: Orbis Publishing Limited, 1979.

———. *Viking Expansion Westward.* London: The Bodley Head Ltd., 1973.

Mattingly, H. *Tacitus: On Britain and Germany.* Harmondsworth, England: Penguin Classics, 1948.

Mauss, Marcel. *A General Theory of Magic.* Translated by R. Brain. New York: Norton, 1952.

Mercer, Beryl and Tricia Bramwell. *The Anglo-Saxon Runes.* Amber, England: Phoenix Runes, 1983.

Musset, L. *Introduction à la runologie.* Paris, 1965.

Napier, A. S. "The Franks Casket." *An English Miscellany Presented to Dr. Furnhall.* London: Oxford University Press, 1901.

Osborn, Marijane, and Longland, Stella. *Rune Games.* London: Routledge & Kegan Paul, Ltd., 1982.

Page, R. I. *An Introduction to English Runes.* London: Methuen, 1973.

———. "Anglo-Saxons, Runes, and Magic." *Journal of the Archeological Association* 27: 14–31.

Palsson, Hermann and Paul Edwards. trans. *Egil's Saga.* London: Penguin, 1976.

Pushong, Carlyle A. *Rune Magic.* London: Regency, 1978.

Ravenscroft, Trevor. *The Spear of Destiny.* London: Neville Spearman, 1972.

Simpson, Jacqueline. *The Viking World.* New York: St. Martin's Press, 1980.

185

Souers, P.W. *Harvard Studies and Notes in Philology and Literature,* vol. 17, 1935; vol. 18, 1936; vol. 19, 1937.

Spiesberger, Karl. *Runenmagie, Handbuch der Runenkunde.* Berlin: Richard Schikowski, 1955.

Stephens, G. *Handbook of the Old-Northern Runic Monuments of Scandinavia and England.* London and Copenhagen: 1884.

———. *The Old-Northern Runic Monuments of Scandinavia and England.* London: Williams & Norgate, 1866–1901.

Storms, G. *Anglo-Saxon Magic.* The Hague: Martinus Nijhoff, 1948.

Syverson, Earl. *Norse Runic Inscriptions with their Long-Forgotten Cryptography.* Sebastopol, California: The Vine Hill Press, 1979.

Thompson, Claiborne W. *Studies in Upplandic Runography.* Austin: University of Texas Press, 1975.

Thorsson, Edred. *Futhark: A Handbook of Rune Magic.* York Beach, Maine: Samuel Weiser, 1984.

———. *Runelore: A Handbook of Esoteric Runology.* York Beach, Maine: Samuel Weiser, 1987.

———. *At the Well of Wyrd: A Handbook of Runic Divination.* York Beach, Maine: Samuel Weiser, 1988.

——— *Rune Might.* St. Paul, Minnesota: Llewellyn Publications, 1989.

Turville-Petre, E. O. G. and Ross, A. "Agrell's 'magico-numerical' Theory of the Runes." *Folklore* 97, 203–13.

Urdiz, Gebu. *Magia delle Rune.* Rome: Edizioni Mediterranee, 1977.

Walgren, Erik. *The Kensington Rune Stone: A Mystery Solved.* Madison: University of Wisconsin Press, 1958.

Whatmough, Joshua. *The prae-Italic Dialects of Italy.* Vol. II. Cambridge, Massachusetts: Harvard University Press, 1933.

Willis, Tony. *Runic Workbook.* Wellingborough, England: Aquarian Press, 1986.

Wilson, David. *The Vikings and Their Origins.* London: Thames and Hudson Limited, 1970.

PRONUNCIATION GUIDE

GERMANIC		SOUND VALUE OF THE GERMANIC AS IN MODERN ENGLISH
1. *Mannaz*	män-näz	*a* as in father
2. *Gebo*	gā-bō	*e* as in play, *o* as in go
3. *Ansuz*	än-sōōz	*a* as in father, *u* as in ooze
4. *Othila*	ō-thēē-lä	*o* as in go, *th* as in thin, *i* as in meet, *a* as in father
5. *Uruz*	ōō-rōōz	*u* as in ooze
6. *Perth*	perth	*e* as in berth
7. *Nauthiz*	now-thiz	*au* as in now, *th* as in thin, *i* as in is
8. *Inguz*	ing-gōōz	*ing* as in spring, *u* as in ooze
9. *Eihwaz*	ā-wäz	*ei* as in play, *a* as in father
10. *Algiz*	äl-gēz	*a* as in father, *g* as in gem, *i* as in meet
11. *Fehu*	fā-hew	*e* as in play, *u* as in hew
12. *Wunjo*	wōōn-jō	*u* as in wound, *j* as in joy, *o* as in go
13. *Jera*	jer-ä	*j* as in join, *e* as in yes, *a* as in father
14. *Kano*	kä-nō	*a* as in father, *o* as in go
15. *Teiwaz*	tā-wäz	*ei* as in play, *a* as in father
16. *Berkana*	ber-kä-nä	*e* as in berry, *a* as in father
17. *Ehwaz*	eh-wäz	*eh* as in yes, *a* as in father
18. *Laguz*	lä-gōōz	*a* as in father, *u* as in ooze
19. *Hagalaz*	hä-gä-läz	*a* as in father, *g* as in give
20. *Raido*	rī-thō	*ai* as in ride, *d* as in though, *o* as in go
21. *Thurisaz*	tu-ri-säz	*thur* as in tour, *i* as in meet, *a* as in father
22. *Dagaz*	thä-gäz	*d* as in then, *a* as in father
23. *Isa*	ē-sä	*i* as in easy, *a* as in father
24. *Sowelu*	sō-wā-lōō	*o* as in go, *e* as in way, *u* as in ooze
25. *Odin*	ō-din	*o* as in go, *i* as in thin

THE RUNEWORKS

Using the Viking Runes and the RuneCards has been, for many people, an exciting adventure in self-discovery. We would be most interested to hear of your experiences with the Oracle and to quote from your letters. If you wish your name withheld, please let us know.

The RuneWorks now publishes a quarterly journal, *The New Oracle: A Journal for the Study of the Oracular Tradition,* featuring interviews with leading-edge thinkers in the fields of anthropology, metaphysics, sacred archeology and healing. It includes articles about the Runes and other oracular traditions, as well as book reviews and innovations in Rune-casting techniques developed by those who use the Oracle.

If you have difficulty finding *Rune Play* (a book in which to record your Rune readings according to the season), *The Book of Runes* (with or without stones), *The Book of RuneCards,* or if you wish to subscribe to *The New Oracle* or be placed on our mailing list, please write to us at:

The RuneWorks
P. O. Box 1320
Venice, CA 90294
(213) 399-3755

We look forward to hearing from you.

There is an old Icelandic Blessing which says *Ver ði þer a ð go ði* . . . May the good come to you . . . May it indeed.

Ralph Blum

ABOUT THE AUTHOR

Ralph Blum received his degree in Russian studies at Harvard University. Following a period in Italy as a Fulbright Scholar, he returned to Harvard, where he did graduate work in anthropology with grants from the National Science Foundation and the Ford Foundation.

Encountering the Runes by chance while doing research in England, he subsequently explored their origins and reinterpreted their meanings in terms appropriate for our time. A writer and publisher, Ralph Blum has been working with and teaching the Viking Runes as a tool for self-counseling since 1980.

He makes his home in Malibu, California.

ABOUT THE AUTHOR

Futhark (*Traditional Order*)

MODERN ENGLISH EQUIVALENT	OLD ENGLISH RUNES	OLD ENGLISH NAMES	GERMANIC RUNES	GERMANIC NAMES	ETRUSCAN	PRE-RUNIC SYMBOLS
f	ᚠ	feoh	ᚠ	fehu		
u	ᚢ	ūr	ᚢ	ūruz		△
þ (th)	ᚦ	þorn	ᚦ	þurisaz		
a	ᚩ	ōs	ᚨ	ansuz	A	
r	ᚱ	rād	ᚱ	raiðō		
k	ᚳ	cēn	ᚲ	kaunaz kēnaz kanō		
g	ᚷ	gyfu	ᚷ	gebō		X
w	ᚹ	wyn	ᚹ	wunjō		
h	ᚺ	haegl	ᚻ	hagalaz		
n	ᛏ	nȳð	ᛏ	naupiz		+
i	ᛁ	īs	ᛁ	īsa-		ǀ
j	ᛄ	gēr	ᛃ	jēra-		
e (ei)	ᛇ	ēoh	ᛇ	eihwaz		
p	ᛈ	peorð	ᛈ	perþ		
z	ᛦ	eolh-secg	ᛦ	algiz		
s	ᛋ	sigel	ᛋ	sowelu		
t	↑	tīr	↑	teiwaz		
b	ᛒ	beorc	ᛒ	berkana-		
e	ᛖ	e(o)h	ᛖ	ehwaz		
m	ᛗ	man	ᛗ	mannaz		
l	ᛚ	lagu	ᛚ	laguz		
ng	ᛝ	Ing	ᛜ	inguz		
o	ᛟ	eþel	ᛟ	opila		
ð	ᛞ	daeg	ᛞ	ðagaz		

Note: While the order of Rune names was to some degree fortuitous, the choice
names was not. A Rune name had to begin with a given sound and poss
mnemonic power